Ancient Africa

A Captivating Guide to Ancient African Civilizations, Such as the Kingdom of Kush, the Land of Punt, Carthage, the Kingdom of Aksum, and the Mali Empire with its Timbuktu

Free Bonus from Captivating History
(Available for a Limited time)

Hi History Lovers!

Now you have a chance to join our exclusive history list so you can get your first history ebook for free as well as discounts and a potential to get more history books for free! Simply visit the link below to join.

Captivatinghistory.com/ebook

Also, make sure to follow us on Facebook, Twitter and Youtube by searching for Captivating History.

Contents

Introduction

Africa is the continent where the first humans were born. They explored the vast land and produced the first tools. And although we migrated from that continent, we never completely abandoned it. From the beginning of time, humans lived and worked in Africa, leaving evidence of their existence in the sands of the Sahara Desert and the valleys of the great rivers, such as the Nile and Niger. Some of the earliest great civilizations were born there, and they give us an insight into the smaller kingdoms of ancient Africa.

Egypt is the main source of knowledge of many neighboring kingdoms that were just as rich and developed. Unfortunately, they were forgotten in time, as other civilizations and kingdoms replaced them as the continent's power bases. Only recently are we rediscovering the might of the Kingdom of Aksum, the political prowess of Kush, and the richness of the mysterious Punt. The early medieval kingdoms of Ghana and Mali are still being researched due to their unique pre-Muslim culture and their own outlook on Islam.

Because of the huge diversity that is the history of Africa, learning about it may be a bit of a challenge. Even though humanity started in that place, we somehow lost interest in it. And although the archaeology programs founded in the mid-20ᵗʰ century helped resolve this somewhat, we are still trying to eliminate the ignorance and racial prejudice of colonial times. Africa keeps many secrets, and they are there, ripe for the picking. The kingdoms discussed in this book serve as an inspiration to future generations to explore what lies below the African ground and behind its oral traditions.

As the home of the many pharaohs, Queen Sheba, Hannibal Barca, and Mansa Musa, Africa deserves our full attention. It has stories to tell us and cultural riches to share with us. Africa is where paganism, Christianity, and Islam left their trails and created a cultural fusion that is unique to the continent. Some modern countries are popular tourist destinations, while others are war-torn lands still unable to industrialize. This polarity of Africa can be traced to ancient times, and the world-shaping events that occurred here need to be studied and understood.

Chapter 1 – The Kingdom of Kush

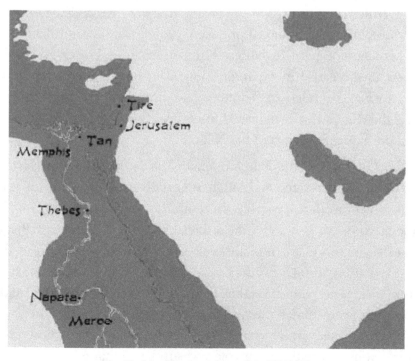

The Kushite Empire at its peak in 700 BCE

https://commons.wikimedia.org/wiki/File:Kushite_empire_700bc.jpg

The ancient history of the Middle Nile Region was constantly determined by the conflicts that arose between Egypt and Nubia. Both kingdoms wanted supremacy over the Middle Nile Region, as it would open trade with the rest of Africa. For Egypt's New Kingdom (16th century–11th century BCE), it was of great importance to keep Nubia pacified so it could use its riches to expand its influence over the territories of the Levant (historical region of Syria). But around 1650 BCE, Lower Nubia came under the control of the Kerma kingdom. Through diplomacy, this kingdom gained control over the trade between Egypt and Africa.

It is this Kerma kingdom that appears in the Egyptian sources as the Kingdom of Kush. The names of the earliest Kush leaders remain unknown, but they had to fight the Egyptian rulers for their dominion. The earliest sources mention Kamose of the Seventeenth Dynasty of Egypt (ruled c. 1555–1550 BCE) fighting the Kush Kingdom; his successor, Ahmose I, picked up where he left off. These rulers began a systematic conquest of Nubia. Kamose secured Lower Nubia, but he was unsuccessful in expanding Egypt farther to the south. It was only during the reign of Thutmose (Tuthmosis) III, around 1460 BCE, that Egypt finally managed to control the southern territories as far as the Fourth Cataract of the Nile.

The Cataracts of the Nile are lengths of the river that are shallow and rapid. Whitewater and small waterfalls occupy some of these areas, which are not navigable. In total, there were six Cataracts, but some are now sunken under the artificial lakes. But even those that do not exist anymore are remembered in history books because they represented natural borders, landmarks, and waypoints of importance. The Nubian regions from the First to the Fourth Cataract of the Nile were under the overseers' governance. Their official title was "King's Sons," which changed under the rule of Amenhotep II to "King's Sons of Kush." Their role was similar to that of a viceroy, and many historians describe them as such. Those who bore this title were not necessarily related to the Egyptian king; they were often elevated to the position due to their endeavors as royal administrators and bureaucrats. During the Middle Kingdom (c. 1975–1640 BCE), Upper and Lower Nubia were a part of Egypt. They shared the same economy, administration, and ideology. At this time, the Egyptians built their temples in the Kush region, devoting them to their gods and pharaohs, such as Re-Harakhte, Amun-Ra, Ptah, Horus, Hathor, and Isis. The worship of a living ruler reached its pinnacle with Ramesses II.

The natives of the Kush regions were Egyptianized to various degrees. The rich families adopted Egyptian names and were allowed Egyptian education. They were even buried in Egyptian-style tombs, which indicates they adopted the religion and the funerary customs of their rulers. At first, scholars believed that all of the natives integrated Egyptian culture into their lives, and this opinion is supported by the material items found in the region. However, with Egypt being the center of the economy, it is natural for everyday items to be of Egyptian origin. The indigenous population had its own customs when it came to mortuary tradition. Even though they used Egyptian equipment, as none other was available, all the evidence suggests they had their own indigenous rites and religions. There are frequent mentions of the goddess *Nhsmks*, as well as other iconographical evidence of various cults that were not of Egyptian origin.

The End of Egyptian Domination

The name Kush was given to Nubia by the Egyptians of the Middle Kingdom. It stands as a designation for the indigenous people of the Nubian region, who were known as the Kushites. However, the term "Kush" can also be found in the personal names of some of the rulers of the region, such as King Kashta, whose name can be translated as "of the lands of Kush." The earliest sources of the history of the Kingdom of Kush are of Egyptian origin. Because of the constant conflicts in the Nubian region, the lands of Kush were those south of the Nile's First Cataract, which needed to be conquered. After the reign of Kamose, these lands were under Egyptian dominion for nearly five centuries (from c. 1550-1069 BCE). Although Nubia was swiftly incorporated into the Egyptian New Kingdom after the initial conquests of Kamose and Ahmose I, the region was still the birthplace of many rebellions. There are constant mentions of various uprisings of the Kush regions from the reign of Thutmose IV (r. 1401-1390 BCE) until Ramesses III (1186-1154 BCE) in numerous sources. Every ruler had to fight the local people to keep control of the region.

The reasons for these rebellions are unknown, but there is a theory that the conflict arose over Lower Nubia's mines, which were rich in gold. The areas of the Fifth and Sixth Cataracts of the Nile were also troubled by conflict, which was probably caused by the political interference of the southern regions that were free of Egypt's dominion. The Kush elite grew stronger in the most southern parts of Egypt-controlled Nubia, around the Napata region. There, after the Egyptian withdrawal from Upper Nubia during the Twentieth Dynasty (1189-1077 BCE), the rule was passed to the local elite. However, it is not clear whether these indigenous rulers had complete freedom or were vassal kings of Egypt. Some historians suggest that it was Ramesses III who withdrew his kingdom from the Napata region all the way to Kawa, which lay on the east bank of the Nile.

Both of these theories are contradicted by the written evidence of Ramesses IX, who collected Nubian tribute and who gifted the agricultural land in the region. Nevertheless, it seems as if the Egyptian administration of the regions south of the Third Nile's Cataract was very weak. The northern regions continued to be under the strong influence of Egypt until the late 12th century, though. During the reign of Ramesses XI (1098-1069), Egyptian dominion reached the southern areas up until the Second Cataract.

There is no evidence that can suggest the withdrawal of Egypt from Upper Nubia was due to the aggression of local rulers. However, it occurred during the decline of the political and economic power of the later pharaohs. At the same time, Egypt abandoned Palestine due to the migration of the Eastern Mediterranean Sea Peoples, who greatly influenced Egypt's central government. With the decline of the Kingdom of Egypt, the ideology of the Nubian regions changed. Suddenly, the populace supported the return of local socio-political structures, or at least what was left of them after five centuries of Egyptian rule. It became impossible for the pharaohs to maintain the hierarchy in Nubia because their economy had suffered. Due to the poor economy, their military power was weakened, and as such, Egypt couldn't afford to quell the Kush rebellions anymore. The permanent economic crisis started with the rule of Ramesses IX. By the time of Ramesses XI, a civil war had erupted, instigated by the conflict between Viceroy of Kush Panehesy and High Priest of Amun Amenhotep. The reason for this conflict remains unknown, but during it, the economic crisis was of such intensity that even the army started looting tombs. Famine followed the war, and the atrocities committed by both the viceroy and the high priest shocked the people of Egypt.

The conflict ended with the rise of powerful men, as Paiankh became the next viceroy of Kush, and Herihor replaced High Priest Amenhotep. The descendants of Herihor would become the rulers of Egypt in what is known as the Twenty-first, Twenty-second, and Twenty-third Dynasties. Their time coincided with the renaissance period that followed, a period when Egypt underwent renovations and recovery after the civil war. However, Panehesy kept Lower Nubia for himself, and Paiankh constantly tried to return these territories under the control of Egypt. The conflict between an ex-viceroy of Kush and the new one ended with a treaty that limited Egypt's authority to the region between the First and Second Cataracts of the Nile. The rest of the southern Nubian territories remained independent.

The descendants of Herihor regained limited control over the whole Nile Valley between the First and Second Cataracts. This brought the gold mines of the Middle Nile Region back under Egyptian control. The members of the royal family were also appointed as the viceroys of Kush, which meant they claimed the rule over all of Nubia, even though it was limited to one region. The last viceroy of Kush, Pamiu, governed the region from 775 to 750 BCE. With the Kushites establishing control over Lower Nubia, the office of the viceroy ceased to exist. By the time of Pamiu, the viceroy's influence was limited only to the temple domains of the region, signifying that the Nubian area under Egypt's control shrank even more. In the following years, the pharaohs would continue with the efforts to regain some of the lost territories because it was this area that controlled the trade with the rest of Africa. When it was clear that Kush was lost to the Egyptians, trade contacts were established. These contacts went as far south as the Sixth Cataract of the Nile, and they are mentioned in both Egyptian and Assyrian sources.

The Unification of Successor States

There is written and archaeological evidence for the continuous depopulation of Lower Nubia from the end of the New Kingdom until the Twenty-fifth Dynasty. However, some scholars believe that the depopulation didn't happen. The illusion was created by the people of Nubia, who started changing their burial practices at this point in history. Many are yet left to be discovered, and there is simply not enough evidence that leads to a unified view on the matter. There are some new promising discoveries, like the necropolis at El-Kurru, which are dated to this period, but much of the work is left to be done, and more sources need to be discovered. Because of the lack of evidence, the period between the 11th century and 8th century BCE remains obscured.

What is evident is the survival of the indigenous chiefdoms, which overlooked the production of goods and its local redistribution. Once the viceregal government collapsed, the native social structure resurfaced. Small-scale polities were created to replace Egypt's government system. The Egyptized elite of the society rose to become leaders, with each creating his own successor state of Nubia. However, the newly created states were bound to become less developed social and economic structures, as they were left to rely on local resources once Egypt withdrew. They had no imperial military help from Egypt either, and they were left to the mercy of their rivals and enemies who surrounded them.

Egypt continued to attack the Nubian region, wanting to reintegrate it into the imperial government. This, and the failing economic administration of the successor states, led to the increased need for the successor states to unify. But it was the lack of natural resources that finally pushed the region to unite. Some regions of Nubia were rich in mines, while others had arable lands. The redistribution of resources had to be brought under a single administration. The El-Kurru chiefdom became the leading political entity of the unification of the Nubian region, as they possessed the gold mines between the Fourth and Fifth Cataracts of the Nile. El-Kurru also held secure routes for the caravans that traded inside Nubia and with the interior of Africa. To be clear, though, the original name of the chiefdom is not recorded. El-Kurru is just the name of the modern village where the town was discovered.

The El-Kurru chiefs traded with Egypt, and they kept peaceful relations with the Egypt-controlled regions of Lower Nubia. There is evidence of material items of both cultures found all over the Nile Valley, which suggests that some kind of trade existed. During the 8th century, the influence of the Kingdom of Kush stretched to the Second Cataract of the Nile, which was where the Egyptian authority in the south ended, but the Kushites did not expand only to the north. The south proved to be of equal interest, as it was the way by which trade with the rest of Africa occurred. It seems that the trade with Ethiopia was well developed, as items made out of ivory and lapis lazuli were found in the tombs of the Kushite chiefs of El-Kurru.

Unfortunately, some regions lack the evidence that would speak about their history before the unification with the rest of the Kushite kingdoms. One such region is the Butana, which was not a part of Egypt, as the Kushites annexed in the mid-8th century. This suggests that the region was independent, but there is no evidence that speaks of its history or culture. The settlement in Meroe contains some of the graves of El-Kurru chiefs, which were dated to before the annexation period. This indicates that the connection between the Kush and Butana region was of much earlier date. Meroe became the political center of the region after the conquest by the El-Kurru dynasty. There is evidence of a marriage between the El-Kurru dynasty and the local princes of the Butana region, which speaks in favor of a peaceful unification rather than conquest. The Meroitic-speaking population of the Butana region was acculturated to the Egyptianized El-Kurru within just a few generations.

The Twenty-fifth Dynasty and the Kingdom of Kush

The El-Kurru dynasty spread its authority from the Butana region in the south to Lower Nubia in the north by the mid-8th century. At this point, the first recorded king of the Kingdom of Kush emerged. His name was Alara, and he ruled a complex state. The Egyptian religion was already accepted among the Kushite leaders to some degree. However, Alara placed his own sister as a priestess of Amun, establishing the first official cult of an Egyptian deity. It is speculated that the trade in gold and exotic animals were what allowed the Kushites to convert from chiefdoms to a complex kingdom. Thanks to its geographical position, the El-Kurru chiefdom had an advantage over the rest of the Nubian states and proved to be the competent leaders of the unification.

This period of the Kingdom of Kush is known as the Napatan period because the kingdom was centered around the city of Napata. However, it is unknown when and how the Kingdom of Kush rose around Napata, as there is no written or archaeological evidence that provides proof. Alara's successor was Kashta, and it is believed that the two Kushite kings were brothers; however, this is just a theory, as no concrete evidence supports this claim.

It was with Kashta that the relationship between the Kingdom of Kush and Egypt tightened. The evidence suggests that Kashta imposed his authority over Upper Egypt peacefully. The descendants of Pharaoh Osorkon III withdrew from Thebes to make room for the growing power of the Kushite king, but they continued to enjoy a high social status in the city and were even buried there. Kashta also managed to place his daughter, Amenirdis I, in the position of the Divine Adoratrice of Amun, a successor to the position of God's Wife of Amun. This title previously belonged to the daughter of Pharaoh Osorkon III, Shepenupet I. The appointment of Kashta's daughter served to prove the legitimacy of the reign of Kashta's successors in Upper Egypt. The appointment of the Divine Adoratrice of Amun symbolized the transition of power from one pharaoh to another. In this case, the appointment of Kashta's daughter meant that he was next in line to become the pharaoh. It also meant that the dynasty beginning with Kashta was legitimate, as it was approved by the god Amun. Amenirdis I guaranteed that Kashta's successors would be legitimate rulers of Egypt.

But why did the Theban princes accept the alliance with the Kushites from the south and the eventual power shift? It was due to the fact that the already-fragmenting Egyptian state was facing an invasion from Libyan chieftains. The Kingdom of Kush would help provide the safety of its southern borders. However, there are no sources that offer an insight into the achievements of Kushite King Kashta. Nothing is known about his activities, either in the Kingdom of Kush or in Upper Egypt. Napata is still a rich archaeological site, and artifacts remain to be excavated. However, the Egyptianization of the Kushites continued under his rule and even intensified. The evidence of this is found in the southern region of the Butana, where Egyptian-style coffins were excavated from tombs. Over the next century, the Kushites adopted Egyptian literacy and used it to articulate the Kushite ideology of power. However, the traditional Kushite social structures continued to exist, and they actually coexisted with Egyptian social relations and concepts.

Kashta probably died in 747 BCE and was buried in the necropolis of El-Kurru in an Egyptian-style pyramid. He was buried with all the Egyptian traditions, even though his tomb was plundered at some point in history. He was succeeded by Piye, who was probably his son, but the relationship between the two remains to be proven.

As it further proves the Egyptianization of the Kush elite, Piye took the five-part title that was similar to the one that belonged to Thutmose III. Pharaoh Thutmose III had conquered Kush, and this new Kushite king, Piye, would, in turn, conquer Egypt and start the Twenty-fifth Dynasty. While Thutmose III was crowned in Thebes, the Kushite ruler of Upper Egypt was installed in Napata, announcing the political shift that was about to happen. In one of his royal speeches, which was recorded on a stela, Piye claimed Amun had appointed him as the king of Nubia so that he could extend the Kushite influence and conquer Egypt. He also announced himself absolute overlord above all other kings. However, in the same speech, he declared that Egypt's political situation wouldn't change as long as all its kings and chiefs recognized his supremacy and paid him tribute.

Another stela from Napata mentioned Piye and his army going to Thebes to gift the temple of Amun. The presence of his army suggests that some kind of conflict between the Kingdom of Kush and Egypt took place in the fourth year of Piye's reign, but it could be that the Kushite king had to defend his borders from the Great Chiefs of the West (probably a threat from Memphis). There are no records that describe the events of the next fifteen years in the Kingdom of Kush, but Assyrian sources speak about their advancement toward Egypt and the appointment of an Arabian tribe at Gaza, which served as the gatekeeper over Egypt. In Egypt, Tefnakht, Prince of Sais, consolidated his power and founded the short-lived Twenty-fourth Dynasty during this period.

At first, Piye recognized the authority of Tefnakht, but when the Egyptian pharaoh attacked Hermopolis, Piye ordered his Kushite forces from Thebes to relieve the city after its rulers appealed for help. Piye's army successfully drew back Tefnakht's forces and laid siege to Hermopolis. Piye decided to leave Napata and take personal control of his army. He triumphed over the Egyptians and entered the city of Hermopolis, where he received homage from the local rulers. Then he marched his forces toward Memphis, where a part of Tefnakht's army was stationed. After the victory there, he received affirmation of his rule at the sanctuary of Ptah. In Memphis, the chief of the Ma (a region of the Nile Delta), Iuput II, submitted to Piye. Next, Piye entered Heliopolis after receiving the submission of its prince, who confirmed his kingship in a ceremony of enthronement. Fifteen local rulers submitted to Piye after this ceremony, and Tefnakht realized he had to start the negotiations. Although Tefnakht agreed to recognize Piye's authority, he remained the ruler of an independent region of the western Nile Delta. Once Piye returned to Napata, Tefnakht assumed the royal title again, breaking his allegiance to the Kushites.

Piye didn't bother with establishing his own administration in the newly conquered regions. He was satisfied with reinstalling local rulers who would take care of the governance but pay tribute to him as vassals. The conquest itself was recorded on the Great Triumphal Stela, which was written by Egyptian literary stylistic rules. Because of this, the stela is not a precise and objective record, but it was a literary work that served to spread the propaganda of King Piye. The stela details the attempt of Pharaoh Tefnakht and his ally Nimlot, the ruler of Hermopolis, to unify Lower and Upper Egypt through conquest, which was thwarted by the efforts of Piye.

The conflict ultimately resulted in the king of Kush becoming the supreme ruler of Egypt. Although local rulers were allowed to keep their title of king, the title of pharaoh now belonged only to Piye. It is not known how many years Piye ruled, but there is no evidence that suggests he returned to Egypt after the conquest.

Piye's successor, Shabaqo (716-702 BCE), moved the capital from Napata to Memphis because of the closing threat of the Assyrians, who, at the time, were under the rule of Sargon II. It is unknown if Shabaqo was Piye's son or brother. Shabaqo tried to annihilate the local dynasties, and he placed Sais and the region of Pharbaitos under his direct control. But instead of completely getting rid of the local rulers, he subdued their authority under the centralized government. The vassal kingdoms were now under the authority of the local governors. However, this would change once Egypt received its first blow by the Assyrians, after which the local dynasties would revert to power.

But during Shabaqo's rule, Egypt and Assyria were fairly friendly. King Yamani of Ashdod, who rose up against the rule of Sargon II, sought refuge in Egypt. However, Shabaqo didn't want to deepen the animosity with Assyria, and in the year 712 BCE, he decided to extradite the asylum seeker to maintain peace. After securing the peace, Shabaqo concentrated on strengthening his dynasty's position in the Egyptian half of his kingdom. To achieve this, he appointed his son, Horemakhet as the high priest of Amun in Thebes. It is possible that Shabaqo felt the need to reinforce his authority over Egypt because his succession wasn't patrilinear as Egyptian tradition demanded. This would mean that he was, indeed, Piye's brother. The Kushite tradition was different, and it allowed for collateral succession (succession by relatives).

Shabaqo died in 702 at Memphis, but his body was moved to his ancestral tomb in El-Kurru. He was succeeded by Shebitqo (705-690 BCE), his son. Although Shebitqo was crowned in Thebes, just like his father, he ruled from Memphis. After all, it was the place where the first kings of Egypt were born and crowned by the gods, which helped to secure his legitimacy as pharaoh.

There is new archaeological evidence that suggests Shebitqo ruled first, not Shabaqo, as previously thought. There is even a theory that the two kings shared the rule at one point, which causes historians even more confusion. The dispute is still ongoing, as it seems that the written and archaeological evidence do not match. The newest conclusion is that Shebitqo ruled before Shabaqo. One of the most convincing pieces of evidence is the style of their pyramids. While Shebitqo's pyramids look more like Piye's, Shabaqo's is closer to the ones owned by Taharqo, who ruled after these two kings. If the pyramid style changed gradually (a theory supported by other archaeological evidence), then Shabaqo surely ruled after Shebitqo. This book follows the guide written by Lazlo Torok, a Kushite expert who believes Shabaqo ruled first.

After the succession, Shebitqo summoned the Kushite army, placing it under the command of his cousin and successor, Taharqo. He decided to confront the Assyrians, who were now ruled by Sennacherib. The assumption is that the Egyptian-Kushite army was defeated in 701 BCE at Eltekeh (in today's Israel) and was forced to return to Egypt. However, the Assyrian king decided to return to his empire, which leaves a dilemma of who actually won. Neither of the armies continued the conquest, and this was the only known military action to occur during Shebitqo's rule. After his death, Taharqo (690–664), the son of Piye, became the king.

The general opinion is that Shebitqo chose Taharqo as his heir apparent because of the Assyrian threat, as the other male representatives of the dynasty were too young. Taharqo ruled in prosperity for the first seventeen years. He built temples in both Kush and Egypt, which were the centers of his administrative power. Trade prospered under his rule, and it spread from Libya and the Levant to the Phoenician coast. However, there were some conflicts, which are attested by the list of captives from the Asiatic principalities. An inscription found at the Sanam temple lists the conquered people, and it even includes Libyans, which might suggest that it wasn't trading but rather military conflicts that created the contact between the two kingdoms.

In 674 BCE, Taharqo's prosperous rule was challenged when the Assyrians attacked Egypt. King Esarhaddon of Assyria made an alliance with Taharqo, and together, they conquered the lands of

Palestine. There, the Assyrian king turned against his ally, for, by this point, he was already on the Egyptian border. Three battles were fought between Taharqo and Esarhaddon, and even though the Egyptians initially won, the Assyrians managed to take over Memphis and sack it. Taharqo was forced to retreat to Thebes in the south. However, his family, including his son, were captured. Taharqo led numerous revolts from the south, but in the end, he proved to be an incompetent ruler who had lost his prosperous and united kingdom at the sign of the first threat.

To quell the unrest in Egypt caused by the actions of Taharqo's rebellions, Esarhaddon set out with his army. However, he died on his way to Memphis in 669 BCE. He was succeeded by his son Ashurbanipal, who decided to annex Egypt. But Taharqo reasserted his power after the Assyrian king's death, and Ashurbanipal was forced to invade the kingdom in 667/666 BCE. In the battle at Pelusium, located in the eastern Nile Delta, the Egyptian army was crushed. Taharqo fled to the south but was pursued by the Assyrians to Thebes. From there, he continued to run farther south, as he was unable to organize a resistance. Ashurbanipal received the submission of the local dynasties of Upper and Middle Egypt. Satisfied, he returned to his capital in Nineveh (Assyria). Taharqo was reduced to the King of Kush, and he remained in his kingdom until he died in 664 BCE.

Taharqo was succeeded by Tanwetamani (or Tantamani, r. 664–656), the son of Shebitqo. During his reign, he organized a series of campaigns, during which he reconquered parts of Upper Egypt. However, Ashurbanipal became aware of his plans, and he sent the Assyrian reinforcement army to defend his possessions there. Most historians agree that the main reason Tanwetamani failed to retake all of Egypt was that he chose to rule from his capital in Kush instead of moving to Memphis, which was closer to the point of conflict. The Assyrians were quick to retake all their Egyptian possessions, and they even sacked Thebes. The Nubian rule of Egypt ended with the

Assyrian conquest, and Tanwetamani was reduced to ruling only the Kingdom of Kush.

The End of the Napatan Dynasty

The nominal rule of Thebes remained in Tanwetamani's hands, but he never returned to Upper Egypt. The Nile Delta was ruled by Psamtik I (664–610 BCE), an Assyrian vassal who founded the Twenty-sixth Dynasty. By elevating his daughter to the position of Divine Adoratrice, he successfully spread his influence over Upper Egypt. Thus, Egypt was reunited. Psamtik I gained Thebes through diplomacy with the Kushites, and Tanwetamani withdrew to Napata.

The relations between Egypt and the Kingdom of Kush continued to develop due to the increased demand for international trade. While there is no evidence of imported goods from Nubia to Egypt, Kushite dig sites are filled with items of Egyptian origin. There is even evidence of conflicts happening between the two states in the area of Lower Nubia and the Red Sea. These conflicts were probably organized against the nomadic tribes of Troglodytes in Egypt's effort to establish control over the trade routes.

For the next few decades, the relationship between Egypt and the Kingdom of Kush remained hostile, despite their connections in trade, and it remained so through the reigns of the next three Nubian kings: Atlanersa, Senkamanisken, and Anlamani. The archaeological and textual evidence of the political state of the Kush Kingdom during this period is sparse. However, one of these rulers decided to change the tradition of burying the royal household members at El-Kurru after he founded a new necropolis at Nuri, where all the future kings would be laid to rest.

In 593 BCE, Pharaoh Psamtik II sent an expedition to Nubia, and even though the reason for his actions is unknown, it is suspected that he wanted better control over Lower Nubia to secure trade routes. But the possibility that he wanted to conquer the Kushites cannot be excluded. It is believed that this Egyptian campaign reached Napata. There is no evidence to suggest the immediate outcome of the conflict, but after this point, the Kushites were no longer welcome in Egypt. The systematic eradication of everything Kushite began, and the statues, names, and inscriptions of the Twenty-fifth Dynasty were destroyed. It seems that Egypt wanted to wipe out the Kush Kingdom from its history.

The campaign of Psamtik II probably happened during the reign of Kushite King Aspelta (c. 600–580 BCE). His reign was overshadowed by a terrible crime in Napata. In the temple of Amun, the names and a figure of the king were erased from two stelae, the Election and Banishment Stelae. Aspelta erected these stelae in the first two years of his reign. The face of the queen mother was also erased, together with the figures of Aspelta's female ancestors. This could mean that Aspelta's legitimacy to the throne was disputed and that the problem lay in the female succession line. Scholars can only speculate on who did this and why, but the general opinion is that Aspelta usurped the throne from an elder relative.

There are no surviving royal inscriptions that can be dated to the period between Aspelta and Irike-Amannote, who ruled at the end of the 5th century BCE. These 150 years are only remembered due to the archaeological findings of the burial sites of the kings and queens at Nuri. However, these tombs were badly plundered, and there are no items that give us enough clues about what the political situation was at the time or even what their relations were like with Egypt. The overall impression of the kingdom's political and economic decline is reinforced by the lack of royal documents, monuments, and buildings dated to this period. However, political continuity is displayed by the ten consequential kings, who lived between the 6th and 5th centuries BCE. They were all buried at Nuri in Egyptian-style pyramids, which means they never abandoned the adopted mortuary religion.

The great Greek historian Herodotus wrote about the southernmost land of Kush in his work, which can be dated to 450–430 BCE. He described the land as inhabited by nomadic peoples, whose rulers produced large amounts of gold, large elephants, various types of trees, and ebony. According to him, the Aethiopians, or Kushites, were very tall, handsome, and long-lived. According to Herodotus, all the lands south of Egypt belonged to Aethiopia (Ethiopia), and he describes the city of Meroe as its capital. The fact that Herodotus even wrote about Kush in this way indicates that Egypt changed its policy toward its southern neighbors. During Ahmose II's reign, trade relations were reestablished, and the Kush Kingdom sent ivory as a tribute. This leads one to the conclusion that Psamtik II may have succeeded in asserting his authority over the region.

During the rule of Persian King Cambyses II (530–522 BCE), the Kush Kingdom came under Persian rule. He conquered Egypt in 525, and in the same year, he invaded Nubia, conquering the lands up to the city of Meroe. Even Xerxes I (486–465) lists the Kushites as one of the peoples under his rule. This fact is supported by Herodotus's writings, in which he describes the Kushite warriors as part of Xerxes's army. Once the Egyptians started organizing revolts against the Persian rule around 486 BCE, the Kushite kings saw an opportunity to regain the territories between the First and Second Cataracts of the Nile. Although the Egyptian rule over the territories between the First and Second Cataracts ceased during the late 5th century, there is no evidence of Kushite military advances. However, the Kushites had some authority over the nomadic tribes that inhabited the lands between the Nile and the Red Sea. This period of the Kingdom of Kush was marked by the long reign of Irike-Amannote (or Amanineteyerike), but it is uncertain if he led his armies to Upper Egypt or if he pretentiously took the title of *Nebty*, "Seizer of the Land," just to show his intentions of an invasion of Egypt.

Irike-Amannote was succeeded by Baskakeren, who only ruled for a short period. Harsiotef ruled next, and he was most likely the son of Irike-Amannote. One of the stelae in the temple of Amun at Napata dedicated to Harsiotef claims he won nine military victories during the first thirty-five years of his reign. His campaigns were recorded as conflicts with the Butana, the desert peoples, Lower Nubia, and

Meroe. In Lower Nubia, he probably fought against the rebels who opposed his rule, while in other areas, he would have fought mostly nomadic tribes. The recorded list of conflicts indicates that, at the time, Kushite authority extended over the territory between the Second and First Cataracts of the Nile. The note beside the Lower Nubia victory entry says that the rebels retreated to Egypt, which might indicate Egypt's involvement so they could regain control of these territories.

Harsiotef was succeeded by an unnamed king, whose efforts to return the royal burial site to El-Kurru suggest there was some kind of dynastical struggle. Nothing is known about this king except that his successor, Nastasen, returned the burial site to Nuri, restoring the dynastical order. The period of the 4th century remains very obscure, and there are no surviving records that cast light on the events in the Kingdom of Kush. However, looking from the perspective of Egypt, there is much to be discovered. During the reign of the Thirtieth Dynasty, in 343 BCE, to be more exact, the Persians returned and conquered the country. Pharaoh Nectanebo II was forced to flee to Upper Egypt, where he received Kushite support and remained in power for the next two years. But Alexander the Great came swooping in next, conquering Egypt in 332 BCE and starting the Ptolemaic Dynasty, which tried to take over the Kingdom of Kush on more than one occasion. In 319/18, Ptolemy I led an attack on Lower Nubia, but his success is not recorded. Egypt must have suffered some internal dynastic problems, as, at the time, the Kushites saw an opportunity to harass its borders.

In 274 BCE, Ptolemy II launched an expedition to Lower Nubia, probably intending to secure the trade routes along the Nile between Egypt and the Kush Kingdom. The Macedonian rulers of Egypt were accustomed to the use of war elephants, which they imported from India. However, it was impossible to import them by such a distance, and Ptolemy needed a new source for his favorite war animal. The only other region that had elephants were the southern regions of the

Kingdom of Kush. But the Kushites didn't know how to capture and train elephants for warfare, and they needed the help of Egyptian experts. However, since there were more diplomatic ways to achieve the elephant trade, the more obvious reason for Ptolemy's expedition to Lower Nubia was its gold mines. Egypt defeated the Kush Kingdom, and Lower Nubia was annexed. However, the Kushites were compensated for the defeat by lucrative trade agreements and the cultural renaissance that followed. Egypt once more established cultural and intellectual contact with the Kingdom of Kush.

The Meroitic Dynasty and the End of the Kingdom

New trade agreements with Egypt brought prosperity to the southern regions of the Kingdom of Kush. From there, exotic animals, as well as other goods, were sold to Egypt and the rest of the known world. However, with the economic strength of the southern parts of the country, a dynastic change was inevitable.

King Arkamaniqo (Arkamani), who ruled in the 3rd century BCE, was the one who transferred the capital from Napata to Meroe. Greek historian Diodorus Siculus records how there was a conspiracy of the southern priesthood to remove Arkamaniqo from the Kushite throne, but he used his knowledge of Greek philosophy to overcome the troubles and slaughter the priests who wished him dead. The story of King Arkamaniqo's coming to the south to dispose of the priests is just an allegory of the moving of the capital and the dynastical change. In reality, Arkamaniqo only transferred the royal burial place to Meroe. However, he was of southern origin, and the choice of his titular name was lent from Ahmose II, who never hid the fact that he usurped the throne, which led to the belief that Arkamaniqo himself was a usurper, hence the dynastical change. The new usurper king was probably part of the new and rich elite society of Meroe, and because of his origins, the dynasty he founded is known as the Meroitic Dynasty. The new dynasty brought prosperity to the kingdom, and even though the south was of special importance due to its trading potential, the kingdom, as a whole, developed exponentially. Meroe and the Butana region did become administrative temple centers, but the fact that Arkamaniqo's successor, Amanislo, continued to build and develop Napata serves as proof that this city continued to be the seat of the kings.

Through increased trade between the Kingdom of Kush and Ptolemaic Egypt, the two cultures continued to influence each other. However, a new trend in art was adopted in the Kush Kingdom. Brought through the Greek contacts of Egypt, Hellenistic art characteristics started appearing in Kushite religious ideology, architecture, and iconography. But the Kushites were also influenced by the African art style, mainly due to the south's economic supremacy. This new African trend enriched the art of Ptolemaic Egypt and continued to expand toward the Hellenistic world in general.

The first conflict between Egypt and Meroitic Kush occurred in the late 3rd century when Upper Egypt revolted against the rule of Ptolemy IV Philopator. The Kushites saw an opportunity to capture Lower Nubia, and it remained in their hands from 207 until 186 BCE. They took the part of Lower Nubia between the First and Second Cataracts, and it appears they had no intention of progressing farther. They just wanted their land back. No military garrisons were found beyond the First Cataract, and no preserved sources mention any intention of conquering Egypt. In 185, Ptolemy V Epiphanes crushed the rebellion and extended his kingdom to the Nile Valley, taking back the lands between the First and Second Cataracts.

During the revolt and its quelling, the trade between the Kush Kingdom and Egypt suffered. The exotic African goods didn't flow to the Nile to be sold to the Hellenistic world. By the early 2nd century, Egypt stopped organizing hunting expeditions to find African war elephants. Instead, they turned back to importing ones from India. However, there is evidence of some diplomatic efforts. Even though Egyptians took back Lower Nubia, the locals were not punished for their role in the rebellion. Instead, they were peacefully integrated into

Egypt's administration, while some of the elite Nubians were even rewarded with positions within the government. The population was subordinate to these native government officials, whom the Ptolemies trusted fully.

In the central regions of the Kingdom of Kush, a new religious and kingship ideology was being shaped. To secure the legitimacy of the new Meroitic Dynasty, Amun transformed into a warrior deity of the desert hunters. The African Butana region's influence is evident here, as the new royal family had originated from there. Even though the royal garments were still heavily influenced by the Ptolemaic ones, traditional components were also incorporated, which held ritualistic meanings. For instance, the Kushite kings' fastening devices were now associated with the Nubian gods Sebiumeker (fertility) and Arensnuphis (hunting), not with the Egyptian warrior god Onuris.

It was as if the new Meroitic Dynasty wanted to separate even more from the old one that had ruled Egypt, for new hieroglyphic and cursive scripts were also invented. The cursive script consisted of only twenty-three symbols, and it was developed for the economic and administrative purposes of the elite and middle social classes. This means that literacy was no longer reserved for kings and priests. Everyone was able to use the new cursive script, and it is thought that even wives and the children of Kushite citizens learned it as well.

The first name that has been discovered in Meroitic hieroglyphs belongs to Queen Shanakdakheto. At first, scholars thought she was a male, as she was the sole ruler on the Kushite throne, but further discoveries of her tomb suggested she was female. Shanakdakheto ruled during the late 2nd century BCE, but it is unknown how she was related to the royal family. Shanakdakheto was also the first known ruling queen of the Kingdom of Kush, with the next one following her at least 100 years later. In the iconography that is dedicated to her, she is represented wearing a feather crown of the Kushite kings and the royal three-part garments. The iconography proves her legitimacy and rule. In one of the depictions, she is accompanied by a male figure, who is dressed more plainly with an ordinary diadem on his head, which symbolizes him as not being a ruling part of the family.

During the 1ˢᵗ century BCE, the Meroitic Kingdom of Kush was involved in a conflict with Rome, which had just conquered Alexandria and Egypt after the suicide of Queen Cleopatra VII. It is believed that the Meroitic Kingdom purposely helped Upper Egypt organize a revolt against the Roman rule to destabilize the region and take over Lower Nubia to the First Cataract of the Nile. However, the result was devastating, as the Roman army entered Kush after they dealt with the revolt in Egypt. Rome conquered Lower Nubia and gave it the status of a vassal chiefdom. The plan was to conquer the whole Kush Kingdom in the future and to annex the Meroitic state. However, the opposition Rome received from Meroe was too great, and Emperor Augustus had to abandon his plans of annexation.

However, only a few years later, Augustus planned two great expeditions. Gaius Petronius was chosen as the new prefect of Egypt, and he was to lead the attack on the Kush Kingdom. However, before the expedition was launched, the Nubians acted first. They crossed the First Cataract and attacked Egyptian towns, where they took prisoners and brought down the statues of Roman Emperor Augustus. The Meroitic attack happened sometime in 25 BCE, while the Roman expedition to Nubia, which served as a counterattack, occurred in the winter of 24 BCE.

At that time, Kushite King Teriteqas, who led the supporting army from the south, died suddenly, and the kingdom was now led by Queen Amanirenas, who has been identified as the previous king's sister. In Roman and Greek texts, she is referred to as "Queen Candace," the Latinized form of "Kandake," but this is just a term that refers to the king's sister. The Meroitic Dynasty was matrilineal, meaning the heirs would be born by the king's blood relatives, not his wife; thus, the kandakes had an instrumental position in society.

Gaius Petronius advanced with his army to Napata, where he ignored Amanirenas's offer of peace, as he took slaves and destroyed the city. However, for some unknown reason, Petronius didn't continue with the conquest of Nubia; instead, he turned back to Egypt.

The loss of Napata didn't diminish the Kushites' will to fight Rome. Queen Amanirenas ordered an attack on a Roman garrison stationed at the border, but Petronius was quick to come back with reinforcements, forcing the Nubians to accept negotiations. The peace talks were held at the Isle of Samos in the winter of 21/20 BCE. The conclusion was the remission of taxes for the Kush Kingdom, as well as the establishment of a border between Egypt and Kush at Hiera Sycaminos (today's El-Maharraqa).

After Queen Amanirenas, the throne was occupied by two more female rulers, Queens Amanishakehto (c. 10 BCE–1 CE) and Nawidemak (early 1st century). The three consecutive female rulers may indicate some dynastic trouble in the kingdom, as it wasn't usual for females to inherit the throne. But during the rule of these queens, the Kushites managed to recover from the conflict with Rome. Once more, the Kush Kingdom entered a period of prosperity, which was reflected in extensive temple building and the increase in the quality of their art. With trade reopened and the successful diplomatic missions that took place, Egyptian influence returned to the Meroitic state. Even the Egyptian hieroglyphic script was in use once again.

The period between the late 1st and mid-3rd century saw an increase and the development of many new agricultural settlements, villages, and caravan stations. The overall impression is that this period was peaceful and prosperous. However, the crisis in the Roman Empire in the mid-3rd century was reflected in the Kingdom of Kush, as economic and political troubles began again. The new Kingdom of Aksum on the southern border was growing powerful and represented a real political threat to Egypt's and Nubia's weakened economies. The warrior tribes of Blemmyae and Noba to the east and southwest started harassing the kingdom's borders.

The last decades of the Kingdom of Kush are poorly documented. The pyramid tombs of the last five rulers show obvious signs of economic decline, as they are less decorated. However, cultural continuity is shown, as even the houses built in Meroe's administrative center show that the kingdom went through some kind of downfall. The people inhabited very small rooms, art stopped being produced, and the temple walls were used as burial grounds. The different types of burials during the second half of the 4th century suggest a new culture was on the rise, which would have coexisted with the Meroitic Dynasty. It seems that the Kush Kingdom was suddenly occupied by a new population that had a completely different cultural, political, and social structure. It is known that the new population was a tribal society built of the warrior elite and semi-nomadic cattle herders. Although it is not known for sure which tribe it was, it is possible it was the Noba, who originated from the western banks of the Nile.

The last known ruler of the Kingdom of Kush was Queen Amanipilade (r. 308-320), but the kingdom continued to exist for at least several more decades after her death. The Meroitic Dynasty disappeared after the attack by the Kingdom of Aksum, which sacked the city of Meroe. A similar fate happened to some other settlements in the area once the Butana lost its role as the administrative and trade center of the kingdom. It remains unknown what happened to the Kingdom of Kush, but the economic fall and the evidence of warfare with the new power in the region, the Aksum, suggest that it was more than one factor that caused its demise. Neighboring Egypt began adopting Christianity, and as a result, the Nubians founded three smaller Christian kingdoms in its territory after the dissolution of the Kush Kingdom: Nobatia, Alodia, and Makuria.

Chapter 2 – The Land of Punt

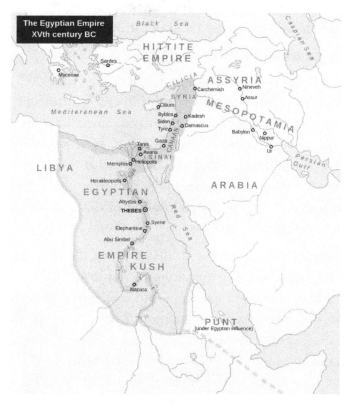

The assumed location of Punt

Andrei nacu at English Wikipedia https://creativecommons.org/licenses/by-sa/4.0/, via Wikimedia Commons https://en.wikipedia.org/wiki/File:Land_of_Punt.png

An ancient African kingdom whose location remains a mystery, the Land of Punt can only be observed through the prism of Egypt, its trading partner. The existence of Punt is known to history only because it was described and depicted in the ancient texts and reliefs of Egyptian rulers. This mysterious kingdom's importance is obvious, as the great pharaohs refer to it as *Ta netjer*—"the land of the gods." Scholars today interpret the name *Ta netjer* in two very different ways, which sheds some light as to where Punt was located. The Egyptians might have named this kingdom "the land of the gods" because it was their ancestral home, where the god Amun installed Egypt's first ruling dynasty. It could also be interpreted as the land in the east, where the sun god rises. The probability of the second theory being correct is increased by the fact that Egypt also referred to Lebanon, another eastern country, as the "land of the gods."

The Location and the People of Punt

There are various theories about where the Land of Punt was located: Morocco, Zambezi, Mauritania, and so on. In reality, nobody knows where the famous mythical land was. Everything known about Punt comes from Egyptian sources, which don't describe the kingdom's geographical position. However, what they do describe is the various goods imported from Punt. Based on that, scholars have concluded that the most probable location of this ancient kingdom is in the Horn of Africa.

The Egyptian texts list products such as ivory, ebony, gold, makeup materials, naphtha, various exotic animals, and gold as being imported from Punt. However, the most important items were aromatic resins and woods, such as myrrh and cinnamon. These items suggest that the mysterious land in the east could be somewhere in Arabia. However, further findings dispute this theory. Archaeologists found a list of the trade partners of Egypt at the temple of Karnak. The list dates back to Pharaoh Thutmose III (r. 1479–1425 BCE) of the Eighteenth Dynasty, and it numbers the kingdoms and their geographical orientations: Kush, Wawat, Punt, Mejay, and Khaskhet. All of these kingdoms were pinpointed in Africa, and their geographical orientation suggests that Punt was the southernmost kingdom that bordered the Red Sea. This location is the Horn of Africa today.

The importance of these imported goods from Punt now becomes obvious. These items, especially the aromatic woods, originated from the region of the Horn of Africa. But the wood could also be imported from Arabia Felix (South Arabia), and this fact made scholars wonder if the Kingdom of Punt may have spread to both shores of the Red Sea. This theory would locate Punt in today's Eritrea and Yemen. Later, scientists conducted a DNA testing of mummified baboon hair found in Egypt, which originated from the mysterious Kingdom of Punt. They found that the DNA profile corresponds to that of Somali baboons. Due to this discovery, historians now believe that today's Somalia was once a part of this ancient kingdom.

The discovery of a Twenty-sixth Dynasty stela from the ancient fortress of Daphnae, near Qanṭarah in northeastern Egypt, shifted the focus of scholars from Arabia to Africa. The stela bears an inscription stating that if it rains in the mountains of Punt, the Nile floods. This would mean that the mountains of Punt should be the Ethiopian Highlands, as it drastically influences the Nile. Since the discovery of this stela, around fifty more inscriptions and engravings that refer to the Land of Punt have been found. None of them mention its exact location. However, they teach us that Punt was not landlocked, as Egyptians traveled to it by boats.

An inscription dating to the Sixth Dynasty tells a story of Pharaoh Pepi II Neferkare (c. 2278/2269-2184/2175 BCE), who dispatched an expedition to retrieve a body of a state official. This official had been killed in the northern desert by the Bedouin tribes while he was overseeing the construction of a ship, which was to set sail to the Land of Punt. This discovery not only confirmed that Egyptians traveled to Punt using the sea, but it also confirmed that it was the Red Sea that was used due to the mention of the northern (Asiatic) desert. Another inscription that was discovered later confirms this theory. This inscription is dated to Pharaoh Mentuhotep III (2010–1998 BCE), and it speaks of another construction of a vessel that was designated to reach Punt along the Red Sea.

Besides the ancient inscriptions that tell us about the various Egyptian expeditions to Punt, there are temple depictions that visualize these expeditions. One has been discovered in the funerary temple of Pharaoh Hatshepsut (1479–1458 BCE) at Deir el-Bahari. According to the depictions of the birth of Queen Hatshepsut, her mother was awakened by the scent of the incense from the Land of Punt. Another depiction in the same temple shows an Egyptian expedition to Punt. The relief shows the recognizable flora and fauna of the land. One of the most recognizable plants is the doum palm, which, even today, grows all over the Somali coast, with the southeast being the place where the concentration of these trees is the highest. To the Egyptians, the doum palm is a sacred plant, and it is no wonder why they wanted to import it directly from the "land of the gods."

Other reliefs from Hatshepsut's temple display the animals and people of Punt. The conclusion is that Puntites mostly traded with short-horned cattle, slaves, and skins of wild animals. They were ruled by their own royal family, and in the time of Hatshepsut, their names were King Parahu and Queen Ati. These are also the only Puntite names known today. The temple of Hatshepsut tried to represent Punt as a land that paid tribute to Egypt, but this is highly speculative, especially since some of the reliefs show the myrrh trees of Punt being cut down by the Egyptians themselves. This is a clear sign that trade occurred, not an exchange of gifts or tribute.

Puntites celebrated the god Amun, but it seems that their main cult was that of the goddess Hathor. Some even speculate that her cult started in Punt. One of the inscriptions found at Al-Qusayr on the Red Sea coast mentions Hathor as the mistress of Punt. All of the goods imported from Punt, whether they were incense, slaves, naphtha, ebony, or animals, were referred to as gifts of Hathor. If Hathor indeed originated in Punt, it would make sense that this mystic land was considered the land of the gods. Hathor is a consort (and mother) to both Horus and Amun-Ra. The two gods were symbols of kingship, and as such, Hathor was the symbolic mother of the Egyptian pharaohs. Some scholars even see Punt as the land where Egyptians originated from. However, there is no evidence to confirm this theory.

King Parahu and Queen Ati, followed by their sons and one daughter, are depicted as they visited Egypt and showed their respect to Hatshepsut. The unusual appearance of Queen Ati draws all the attention. She is represented with a rugged face and an extremely strange body, which modern doctors diagnose as gluteal and femoral obesity and hyperlordosis. Some claim other diagnoses such as elephantiasis or steatopygia. However, without a mummy to conduct proper research, medical experts can only theorize as to why Queen Ati was depicted as such. A newly discovered pathology combines several diagnoses, such as neurofibromatosis, lipodystrophy, Proteus syndrome, and familial obesity. This pathology was named Queen of Punt Syndrome, as the person having it would look similar to Queen Ati's depiction. However, the queen of Punt is, so far, the only known person to have it.

Flora and Fauna of Punt

One of the main items Egyptians imported from Punt was ebony. Products made of ebony, such as ornamental pieces or even sarcophagi, that were found in Egyptian tombs were analyzed, and the results confirmed the suspicion that their origin was from Punt. The particular species of ebony wood found in the tombs is Dalbergia melanoxylon. This type of wood is native to Eritrea, Ethiopia, and Sudan. In Somalia, ebony is very limited today. However, archaeological findings suggest that the situation was quite different in the past. In fact, in the past several millennia, Somalia's vegetation and animal life have drastically changed. The remains of a crocodile were found in the Hargeisa valley, an area with a unique climate. Although it is a dry geographical region today, it is not hot. But the crocodile remains suggest that there was a swamp in the area at some point in the past. The area still grows ebony, locally known as "Kolaati," but to a limited extent. If the area was once a swamp, the possibility is high that ebony was abundant here.

The most important item imported to Egypt from Punt was certainly frankincense. Queen Hatshepsut sent a fleet of five ships to Punt to fetch this scented resin, as it was one of the most important items in Egyptian sacred rituals. She ordered her people to bring not only the resin but also the living saps of the trees, so they could be planted in Egypt. The relief in Hatshepsut's temple depicts thirty-one heavy trees being carried by four to six men. If the Egyptians and Puntites indeed carried the trees to the ships, the Land of Punt must have been very close to the sea.

Ancient texts, among which is the *Periplus of the Erythraean Sea*, specify the region of Somalia between Bandar Qasim and Cape Guardafui as the center of frankincense production and export. The ancient city of Opone, a familiar trade center used by Egyptians, Romans, Greeks, Persians, and even Indians, occupied this region. Since the location of Oppone corresponds to the probable location of the mystical Land of Punt, many scholars believe that they were the same. The *Periplus of the Erythraean Sea* testifies that the frankincense of the highest quality was produced in the laurel grove of Acannae, which has been identified as today's Alula Lagoon in the northernmost point of Somalia.

Just as with the flora of Punt, the fauna was depicted in the ancient Egyptian reliefs of the temples and tombs. One such depicted animal that makes scholars believe the Land of Punt was in Africa is the giraffe. This animal is specific only to Africa, and although they were imported in various other lands, it is highly unlikely that Egyptians would have bothered describing the giraffes of Punt if they were not native to the land. However, ancient Greek texts reveal that giraffes used to roam not just Africa but also the area between Arabia and Syria.

One animal depicted in the reliefs has greatly puzzled scholars. In the depiction of Punt in Hatshepsut's temple, they found a relief of a rhinoceros with only one horn. These are native to the regions of the Eastern Himalayas, while Africa is the home of the two-horned rhinoceros. Some even thought this was enough evidence to search for the Land of Punt in India. However, the relief is badly damaged, and it is not possible to say if the animal used to have two horns. There is also a possibility that one-horned rhinoceros used to inhabit some areas of Africa but went extinct. In the end, it could also just be the error of an artist who didn't bother to add a second horn to the representation of the animal.

Other animals that populated the Land of Punt were fish and marine animals, among which is saltwater lobster. Because of this, scholars are confident enough to imagine Punt as a location with access to the sea. However, some of the fauna species represented on the walls of the temple belong to freshwater habitats. But this was easy for biologists to explain. The represented animals are catfish and a freshwater turtle. Both of these animals are noted to venture to the sea occasionally, which could explain their existence among the depicted seawater creatures.

One more animal posed a challenge for Egyptologists. It seems that there was a strange kind of bird imported to Egypt from Punt. At first, they thought the bird was a crane. However, it only showed the backside of the bird. Later on, another relief was discovered on a nearby wall with the image of the same bird, and this time, the angle was much better. Due to the distinctive feathers on the head, the bird was identified as the secretary bird. This is a large (4.2 feet) terrestrial predatory bird that, to an unskilled eye and observed from an odd angle, could indeed look like a crane. The bird is native to Africa and is nonexistent in the Nile region.

But it wasn't only the images of the animals that were analyzed. Although baboons were represented on various reliefs in the temples and tombs of Egyptian kings and queens, archaeologists have also found mummified remains of baboons in one of the tombs in the Valley of the Kings. The pair of animals were sent to the British Museum, where they were genetically tested to find out their origin. The baboons' oxygen isotopic values matched with those of living baboons native to Eritrea and Ethiopia, ruling out Yemen and Somalia. However, repeated genetic testing results were slightly different. The conclusion was that the baboon mummies correspond genetically to the modern baboons of Somalia and both Eritrea and Ethiopia.

The People of Punt

In the tomb of Rekhmire, who was the vizier of Pharaoh Thutmose III, the Grand Procession Mural was discovered, which depicts foreign envoys submitting tribute to Egypt. The top row of the painting shows the Puntites with several red-skinned people who strongly resemble Egyptians. But the row continues with three black-skinned figures and prognathous facial features. This means that the Puntites were of both Hamitic and Negroid types of people. On the mural, there is nothing of the distinct social or legal status of these types of people, and the general belief is that they were all representatives of the same diplomatic mission from Punt. After all, the region where it is believed legendary Punt used to be is still inhabited by Nilotic and Hamitic peoples.

However, scholars who believe that the Land of Punt solely occupied the Arabic shore of the Red Sea believe that the mural's Nilotic figures represent the slaves of the Puntites, as there is no evidence of this type of people ever being indigenous to Arabia. The Nilotic and Bantu people of Eritrea and Ethiopia, as well as Somalia, have a long history of representing the bulk of the slave class in the Horn of Africa. There are even ancient texts describing the capture of slaves from the areas bordering Sudan and the African Great Lakes region. But that evidence is not enough to claim that Negroid peoples were strictly a slave class. There is textual evidence of racial dichotomy in the area of Ethiopia, which dates back 3,000 years ago. The text, which was discovered in 2013, describes the kings of the ancient Eritrean Kingdom of Da'mat as rulers of both red and black people.

But later, during the Kingdom of Aksum, which spanned over the territories of Eritrea and northern Ethiopia, the terms *saba qayh* (red man) and *tsalim barya* (black slave) were coined. This would mean that the period between 100 and 940 CE was when slavery bloomed. However, there is simply no evidence that would suggest that the social picture of the Land of Punt was similar to that of the Kingdom of Aksum.

What is known about the Puntite slaves comes directly from the Egyptian texts. Several preserved sources speak of Punt exporting Pygmy slaves. Harkhuf, the governor of Upper Egypt during the reign of Pharaoh Pepi II, wrote in his autobiography how he brought a dancing Pygmy as a gift for the child king. He describes how he acquired this Pygmy from the Puntites. He also remembers that another pharaoh had a dancing Pygmy brought to him by the Puntites at an earlier date.

The testimony of Harkhuf made archaeologists wonder where exactly the Puntites got Pygmy slaves. The Pygmy tribes had been concentrated in Central Africa, and it seems that the Puntites traveled deep inside the continent to find them. The excavations performed in the area of northwestern Somalia provided evidence that the people of Punt traveled to the Congo Basin and the Mashonaland gold mines. There, they had access to both slaves and gold, but it remains a mystery if they acquired both by force or by trade.

There are records that mention Pharaoh Pepi II called his Pygmy slave a dwarf, which made historians wonder if these slaves were just individuals from the Horn of Africa who suffered dwarfism or maybe were simply short-statured people. It is also a possibility that Pygmies were not really from Central Africa but rather an indigenous people of Punt. However, research done on modern peoples of Egypt showed a significant number of paternal lineage B-M60 haplotypes among individuals. This DNA haplogroup is commonly found among the peoples of Central Africa, and it is significantly concentrated among the Pygmies. However, this DNA haplogroup doesn't exist in the remains of ancient Egyptians or Sudanese, which leads us to believe that modern individuals who carry it are descendants of the Pygmy slaves of Egypt.

The ethnic name for the Puntites in Egypt was Berber, and it was wrongly assumed in the past that the term bears the same meaning as ancient Greek barbarians (i.e., non-Greeks). Hieroglyphs dating from the time of Queen Hatshepsut refer to the Puntites as "brbrta," and scholars believe that the name is nothing more than the onomatopoeic imitation of the language of Punt. Since Egyptians couldn't understand their language, to them, it sounded like the repetition of the sounds bar-bar or ber-ber. The *Periplus of the Erythraean Sea* describes the areas of northern Somalia, Eritrea, and northern Sudan as the region where the "Berbers" lived. Even the ancient Greeks referred to these territories as "Barbaria," as in "the land of Berbers." In modern times, some of the cities and towns of northern Sudan and northern Somalia still carry the old epithet *Barbaroi* or *Berber* in their names, such as Berbera in Somalia.

Egyptian Homeland?

Even though the Egyptians did not speak the same language as the Puntites, there is evidence that strongly suggests ancestral relations between the two kingdoms. When representing the individuals of foreign lands, Egyptians would always make their figures smaller or caricatured. But when it came to the visual representation of the Puntites, Egyptians would paint them as they painted themselves, even with similar clothes. The only additional feature Puntites had in these paintings was a small beard, which was incredibly similar to the beards often found on the depictions of Egyptian deities.

Another difference between the Puntites and other non-Egyptian nations was their representation in Egyptian hieroglyphic texts. There was a very distinctive symbol the ancient people of Egypt used when they were talking about a foreigner or a foreign land. Whenever Punt is mentioned, this symbol is absent. This led to the conclusion that the Land of Punt was at least seen as equal to Egypt, if not the same.

More similarities between the two cultures can be observed in religion. At the beginning of the chapter, the phrase *Ta netjer*—"the land of the gods"—was mentioned. Historians speculate that this phrase could mean more than just the land to the east. The Egyptian legends of ancestry speak about them coming from the Red Sea coast. The same legends also talk about the gods Horus and Hathor coming from *Ta netjer*. Hathor was sometimes referred to as the "Lady of Punt."

Another Egyptian god, Bes, was often depicted as a giant barbaric deity eating baboons. Those same baboons were described as coming from the Land of Punt in the temple's hieroglyphs at Deir el-Bahari. So, it seems that the Egyptians remembered their origins as natives to Punt. However, their settlement in Egypt must have happened during some remote period, as they lost the ability to understand the language of Punt. But even though Hathor is believed to have come from the Land of Punt, it doesn't mean that she was worshiped as a deity by the Puntites. However, in northern Somalia at the Laas Geel site, ancient rock art was discovered that seems to depict people of the region worshiping a deity similar to Hathor, if not the same. If the location of the Land of Punt was in the area of today's Somalia, this could serve as proof that the Puntites and Egyptians shared religious connections.

Besides cultural ties between Egypt and Punt, there might even be biological ones. If the Land of Punt was in the area of today's Somalia, Eritrea, Ethiopia, Sudan, and the Arabian Peninsula, simple DNA testing shows connections of the inhabitants of all these areas with the modern Egyptian people, who are linear ancestors of ancient Egyptians.

But the DNA of the ancient remains of Egyptians perhaps holds the secret of their ancestry. In 2013, the first genetic study of Egyptian remains was done. Five mummies dating from the late dynasties to the Ptolemaic rule provided the necessary DNA material. One of the mummies gave astonishing results. It showed the presence of haplogroup I, which strongly suggests an origin from West Asia. This haplogroup is extremely rare, and even in ancient times, it occurred only in 5 percent of the overall population of Egypt. It was mostly concentrated in the area of the Kingdom of Kush. Haplogroup I is even rarer today, as only three individuals who carry it have been identified. And the shocking fact is that two out of the three individuals carrying this specific gene set are found in Somalia, while the third one is from Iran. Other genetic studies were done, and they all showed a strong connection between ancient Egyptians and the modern-day inhabitants of Somalia.

Chapter 3 – Carthage

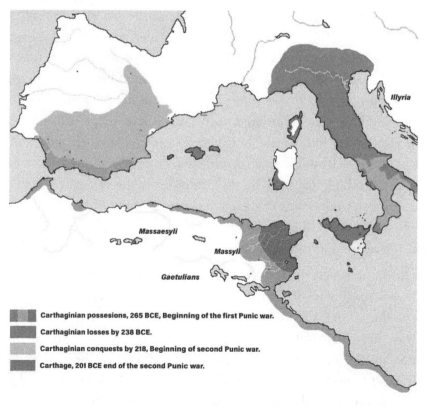

Carthage's dominion during different points in history

https://commons.wikimedia.org/wiki/File:Carthaginianempire.PNG

Many of the great cities in the ancient world have achieved such levels of fame and prosperity that they have mythological stories of their founding. Carthage was no different.

According to the legends, in 831 BCE, the king of Tyre, Mattan I, decided on his deathbed to divide his kingdom to his two heirs. Pygmalion, his son, was to receive one half of the kingdom, and his daughter Dido (sometimes referred to as Alysa) would get the other half. As the story goes, his subjects weren't happy about his decision. They probably worried that dividing the territory under two different rulers would lead to chaos instead of prosperity, so they protested. Thus, Pygmalion became the new king of Tyre, and he quickly began to eliminate everyone with the potential to oppose him.

His sister was the most obvious threat, so she planned to leave the city with all the allies she could muster on the pretense that she did not want to rule over half of the kingdom. She convinced him that she was no threat by asking him to allow her to live at his court. The only reason this sounded plausible to Pygmalion was that he had assassinated his sister's husband, as he was a high priest who opposed him. Her asking him to give her permission to live at the palace after her husband's death eliminated any suspicion of treachery. The king was also looking forward to this change in circumstance because Dido's move to his court would mean that she would bring all the gold that her late husband had accumulated. So, he happily sent her all the help she needed to move her possessions and settle at the palace.

Dido, however, had deceived her brother. She instructed the retainers to move all her belongings to a ship. As soon as they boarded the boat, she dropped several bags into the sea, claiming that it was her husband's gold and other precious treasures, then convinced the retainers to remain aboard and leave the city of Tyre with her. Otherwise, the king would have them killed for losing all that gold. They all agreed and waited for Dido's noble allies to join her on the ship before leaving the harbor. Once everything was prepared, they lifted anchor and sailed to Cyprus.

Once they arrived in Cyprus, they met with another ally, the high priest of the temple of Astarte (equivalent to Venus or Aphrodite). He pledged his loyalty to Dido on the condition that he kept his title and position within his family forever. An agreement was struck, and the high priest gifted eighty of the temple's prostitutes. They were meant to be taken as wives by Dido's companions so that they could start a future settlement of their own.

The exiles left Cyprus and continued their journey to Africa. Their next stop was Utica, a colony where citizens from Tyre had settled. According to legend, it was ruled by King Hiarbas. Dido and her followers were welcomed at first, but when they wanted to purchase land for themselves, the king only allowed them as much territory as could be measured with a single ox hide. Hiarbas was cautious, and he didn't want to risk giving the exiles too much of his territory. But according to the myths, the exiles cut the hide into one long strip and used it to measure a great piece of land. The king had to keep his promise, and thus, the territory was granted to them. This piece of land would soon become known as Carthage. Historical records aren't clear about the true circumstances and the year of the city's founding. Surviving sources point toward the period between 846 and 816 BCE.

The city quickly became popular as more and more colonists started moving to it. Trade was steadily developed together with infrastructure. The prosperity of Carthage made the king of Utica jealous, and he threatened to declare war. However, nobody wanted a war, so the exiled people of Tyre forced Dido to forge an alliance through marriage. The noblemen claimed that they would lead the city to ruin if Dido did do anything to place it in jeopardy. As a result, Dido had no choice but to agree, although she did have one demand. She ordered the people of Carthage to build a large pyre so that she could bring sacrifices to the gods to keep her husband's spirit at peace with this new marriage. The people agreed. However, the first queen of Carthage had different plans. As soon as the fire was lit, she climbed on the pyre and stabbed herself with a sword, declaring that she was joining her husband in death.

Of course, the legend of Carthage and Queen Dido is impossible to verify, and it is highly unlikely to have happened. It is quite a romantic story of treachery and love, though. The first source that mentions the story is dated three to four centuries after Carthage was built, and the first full depiction of the myth comes from a Roman historian who lived in the 1st century BCE. However, we can be sure that some parts of the stories are grounded in fact because there is evidence of Tyrian influence and importance in the city of Carthage.

The Early Days

A depiction of the city of Carthage

The myth that lies at the foundations of this city tells us that the Greeks didn't see Carthage as an ordinary trading post or an unimportant town built by colonists. Its original name in Phoenician was Qart Hadasht, which translates to "New City." This is already enough evidence to confirm that it wasn't just any old settlement. Quite the contrary, in fact. Carthage was built in one of the most important locations in the entire area. It stood at the intersection between two major trade routes: one led from Spain to the Levant, and the other led to Tyre. It also opened up the way to Italy and the entirety of Greece. There were many trade posts, markets, and towns founded on these trade routes, so Carthage was strategically positioned.

During the 8th century BCE, Carthage was already a renowned city where trade was booming. Many Greek and Italian objects, especially pottery, were discovered in parts of the settlement. Ceramics originating from the early days of Carthage were also found in Pithecusa (an ancient city in Italy), showing that the city was already exporting its local production. While the northern trade route had the most to offer, Carthage took advantage of the metals that were brought in by traders traveling between the Levant and Spain, and the city quickly developed into a booming trade center.

In the following two centuries, Carthage developed itself further by becoming a manufacturer of luxury items. At the very beginning, luxury goods were brought from Egypt and the Levant, but with the booming economy, tradesmen and fine craftsmen moved to the new city. This led to a quick population increase, so much so that Carthage could no longer produce enough food to sustain itself. Other colonies started being built in the region to take advantage of new agricultural lands and to extract ore from the mountains. All regional focus was placed on sustaining and developing Carthage into an economic power of great importance.

As Carthage became a prosperous city thanks to its wealthy class of merchants and traders, most of the political and administrative decisions were left to the elite of the trading class. The wealthiest of the merchants were the ones with the most influence. At the time, the Greeks wrongly noted that the city was being governed by an aristocracy that consisted of several kings. However, this was wrong, as the city wasn't ruled by a monarchy at the time. The most powerful merchants had full control of the city, including its military, but they were no kings.

The reason for this confusion is thought to be found in Dido's foundation myth. The elite used the story of the queen that had no children as a way to make their oligarchic rule legitimate. Carthage kept some of its Tyrian heart, but they quickly began to carve their own history by aiming to become a wealthy power with its own way of doing things.

The Rise to Power

573 BCE proved to be the year of opportunity for Carthage, for this was the year when the kingdom of Tyre had to admit defeat at the hands of Nebuchadnezzar, the king of Babylon. Tyre was under siege for thirteen years at that time, and the only chance the city had was to sign a peace treaty. Next to this massive defeat, which had occurred to one of the major economic powers in the region, there was another factor that affected the entire area. Silver decreased in value due to its overabundance. The territories in the Near East were producing and exporting too much silver to the Mediterranean shores. This led to an economic crisis, so many Tyrian colonies were abandoned. With Tyre and many of its colonies on a terrible decline, room was made for Carthage to expand.

The city of Carthage was barely affected by this crisis because it didn't rely as much on the trade with the Levant and the rest of the Near East. Italy and Egypt were the biggest players in the Carthaginian market. The Spain-Levant trade route was an important shipping lane for metal traders, and traffic quickly went down with the price of silver. As Tyrian shipping declined and its colonies abandoned, Carthage could now dominate.

Some ancient historians, especially of Greek and Roman origin, seemed to have been biased against the Carthaginians, as they sought to portray them as aggressive imperialists. However, 6th-century Carthage focused mostly on trade. Around half of their food and other basic supplies came from imports. Although there are some archaeological signs of trouble in Sardinia, where Carthage founded two new cities, we have to look at this evidence with a touch of skepticism. Most testimonies of Carthage's military expeditions come from Roman historians that lived after the events they depict. In fact, most of the stories of aggressive conquest come from the time of the Punic Wars when Rome fought against Carthage (264- 146 BCE). So, we can't be sure about the Romans' objectivity. The signs of conflict found in Sardinia don't conclude that the Carthaginians conquered the territory. The island may have been fought over by the local tribes inhabiting it or by other Phoenicians trying to establish a foothold there.

The same historical sources that depict Carthage as an aggressive power seem to blame them for the fall of the Tartessian kingdom in today's southern Spain. This land was rich in metals, and due to their trade route with the Levant, they became an important trade partner of Carthage as well. The Carthaginians had nothing to gain from warring with them because they were already benefiting from their partnership. Instead, the fall of the Tartessian kingdom is attributed to the fall of the value of silver that led to the economic crisis mentioned above. The wealthy aristocracy that ruled over the Iberian kingdom lost their main source of wealth, which led to conflict and chaos. The kingdom collapsed due to internal struggles ignited by a severely declining economy, not due to military invasions.

Once a power vacuum was created by the conditions in Tyre and southern Spain, Carthage simply took over as the main economic player in the region. Due to their conflict with Rome, as well as the new Carthaginian colonies they established in Sardinia and on the Iberian Peninsula, they may have been seen by ancient historians as invaders bent on controlling the region from an economical and administrative point of view. Whatever the case, other kingdoms and city-states fell due to their struggles, and Carthage was there to take the reins and forge its own path.

Expanding into Africa

Carthage imported a lot of its food from other kingdoms, but with its prosperous expansion during the 6th century, they started relying less on imports. The most drastic change was when they expanded into Africa and started dominating the north. In today's Tunisia, they developed a diverse system of agriculture that was irrigated through springs and canals.

The Carthaginian diet became far more diverse. They consumed several types of grains, vegetables, fish, fruit (such as figs, olives, watermelons, plums, peaches, and almonds), and a wide variety of meat, which came from pigs, cows, chickens, goats, and sheep. The average Carthaginian had a much more diverse diet than the citizens of other kingdoms and empires.

However, the greatest change occurred during the 5th century when they continued expanding into Africa, mainly to today's northern and western Libya. This was when Carthage started becoming a renowned agricultural power in the Mediterranean region, as they would export olive oil and a famous sweet wine that was made from raisins. In the following two centuries, Carthage developed many new techniques in cultivation, irrigation, pruning, and even started using fertilizers.

Colonialism and Conflict

During this period, namely between the 6th and 4th centuries, Carthage hadn't yet achieved imperial status. Even though it was stretching its colonial might into Northern Africa and the entire Mediterranean region, it was still just pursuing its economic goals. Through its influence, many of the other Phoenician colonies started adapting the Carthaginian culture, as well as the Punic dialect that was spoken in Carthage. These colonies also started abandoning the tradition of cremating their dead in favor of burials, which were performed in Carthage.

Carthage continued to expand by building new colonies, to where their excess population would move. Many of the new settlements were fortified to serve as secure marketplaces for the tradesmen that traveled between the agricultural settlements. This expansion included Sardinia, where agriculture was developed to suit the economy of the new Punic kingdom.

The relations between Sardinia and Carthage brought nothing but prosperity, as new imposing office and administrative buildings were built in the Sardinian towns. However, Carthage didn't rule directly over the island. All of Sardinia's cities had their own system of government, and the influence of Carthage was strictly economic and cultural in nature.

While Carthage continued developing the island of Sardinia and building new fruitful endeavors, they sent a military expedition to the island of Sicily in 483. The troops were sent at the request of the ruler of the city of Himera, Terillus, who had been exiled from his city by an invading force from Syracuse. Syracuse was another city in Sicily, but it was ruled by Gelon. Both cities were ruled by the Greeks, but Gelon launched a campaign to take control of the entire island with him as the sole ruler. The Carthaginian elite had a good relationship with the island, but they were forced to act because the western parts of Sicily were vital for the economy of Carthage. However, Hamilcar I, the most powerful man in Carthage at the time, didn't wish to send an official military force in the name of the government. Instead, he opted to create a private army, which was mostly formed from mercenaries who came from all the states in the Mediterranean.

The army arrived on the island in 480 BCE, and it marched directly to the city of Himera. Hamilcar led the army himself, hoping to surprise the city defenses; however, their enemy managed to intercept several letters discussing the plans of the Carthaginians. Hamilcar was ambushed and killed in battle alongside most of his army. The few survivors fled to Carthage and warned the city of what had happened in Sicily. The Carthaginians were now worried that Gelon might attack them, so they began a campaign of diplomacy to seek peace. Ambassadors were sent to Sicily to negotiate a treaty with

Damarete, who was Gelon's wife. The campaign was successful; however, the entire affair was portrayed as a defeat for Carthage at the hands of the ruler of Syracuse.

Carthage had to pay for the war costs and suffered some humiliation, but other than that, nothing really changed for the citizens. They were no longer afraid of an invasion, and the same wealthy merchants continued to rule over the city. However, reforms were made in the system of government, administration, and military. Carthage didn't suffer any economic problems, or, if they did, they were of small significance. But the Carthaginians wouldn't send a new military expedition into Sicily for another half a century, even though they did have the chance to do so. Syracuse was an old enemy of Athens, and the Athenians offered Carthage the chance to forge an alliance against the Sicilians. Carthage refused and chose to respect the peace treaty while continuing to improve its economy and friendly relations with the other Greek city-states.

Carthage didn't make any kind of military move against the island of Sicily in the seventy years that had passed since their defeat. This changed, however, when Segesta, a Sicilian city, entered a conflict with another city called Selinus, as Carthage decided to help. However, this help wasn't being offered to Segesta out of a feeling of brotherhood. To understand why, we have to take a look at what happened in the year 478, as this was the year that Gelon, the man who had defeated the Carthaginians, passed away. As a result, Syracuse lost a great deal of power. Many Sicilian cities started fighting, and this led to failing economies and abandoned towns and settlements. The chaos lasted until 410, which was when Syracuse began to rise again.

Carthage did not want to see a reborn Syracuse dominating over the island, and even though the cities of Segesta and Selinus were unimportant to the Punic kingdom, they provided an excuse to interfere with the island. Carthage, at this time, dominated the Mediterranean trade, and they couldn't risk any challengers. Their goal was to defend their economic and political position in the region.

However, it is entirely plausible they had other motives for getting involved. Although Carthage was still powerful and well respected, the defeat they suffered at the hands of Gelon still stung them.

The elders who ruled over Carthage voted to send aid to Segesta, and as a military leader, they chose Hannibal Mago (not to be confused with the famous general Hannibal Barca), who was the grandson of Hamilcar I, the general who was killed in the Battle of Himera. The expedition was carefully planned, and to avoid intervention from Syracuse, ambassadors were sent to ask them to remain neutral. Selinus didn't ask for help from Syracuse either, even though they were allies, so, therefore, Syracuse could maintain its neutrality in the conflict. However, once Selinus was defeated in a battle against the mercenaries hired by Segesta, they fled to Syracuse to ask for their help. Aid was granted, and the war between Carthage and Syracuse became inevitable.

Hannibal gathered his army, and in 409, he sailed to Sicily to march on Selinus, together with his allies. The city walls were weak and didn't stand a chance against the siege engines, but the defenders tried to hold out for as long as possible, hoping that reinforcements would arrive. The Carthaginian army pushed through the defenses, and in the city's marketplace, they defeated the remaining forces. Hannibal was victorious, and the city was taken. However, Hannibal wasn't satisfied with just conquering Selinus. He pressed on to Himera to avenge his grandfather's defeat and take the city.

The plan was to use the same strategy. However, the defenders of Himera decided to face their invaders on the battlefield, and they attacked the Carthaginian forces. A fleet arrived from Syracuse to support the Himerans, but Hannibal's forces outnumbered them, and they forced the defenders to retreat to the city. The Himerans began evacuating the citizens on the ships that came from Syracuse, and the remaining defenders were forced to hold the city until more ships could arrive for them. Unfortunately for the defenders, they only lasted for three more days.

Ancient historian Diodorus recorded that Hannibal was more ruthless with the people of Himera. While Selinus's walls were destroyed and many buildings burned to the ground, Himera was nearly completely destroyed, temples included. The Carthaginian general gathered his prisoners of war, took them to the place where his grandfather was defeated, and executed them. According to Diodorus, he slaughtered 3,000 men.

The island was at the mercy of Hannibal, but he did not continue his campaign against Syracuse, even though they were offering military and naval assistance to Himera and Selinus. The general's main goal was to wipe the shame that Carthage had felt seventy years before when his grandfather was defeated. After his success, Hannibal paid the mercenaries who fought for him and went back to Africa. But this wasn't the end of Carthage's involvement on the island.

Only two years later, a new military campaign had to be launched because of a rebelling general from Syracuse, who was attacking several settlements. Carthage answered the challenge, but it was not in the way ancient historians like Diodorus portrays. Carthage is often depicted as an invader set upon conquering the island of Sicily with its military might, but that wasn't true. Various inscriptions have been found in the Greek city-states that depict Carthaginian diplomats being welcomed to a number of cities where they sought to form alliances. Furthermore, in the case of the Syracusan general, Carthage first sent envoys to analyze the situation by entering discussions with the leadership from Syracuse and other cities. In any case, Carthage assembled a new army and dispatched Hannibal, together with a young officer named Himilcar, to lead it.

The new expedition didn't start well because the army was ambushed while sailing to Sicily. A number of ships attacked them, destroying several Carthaginian ships before they could reach land. Once ashore, Hannibal led the troops to Acragas, a Greek city in southern Sicily. More misfortune followed, as the army was afflicted by the plague, and many soldiers died. Hannibal himself contracted the plague and died that same year, 407. Himilcar was now the sole leader of the Carthaginian forces, and he continued fighting the Syracusans for two years until the advantage was finally on his side. By 405, he had lost more than half of his men, but due to the strategic positions he won, he was able to offer Syracuse the chance of opting for peace. Carthaginian dominance over the island was now ensured, as several of the cities that went against Carthage had accepted to pay them tribute in exchange for peace.

With a solid economic and political foothold in Sicily, Carthage began investing in building new cities and settlements across the island. Carthaginian immigrants flocked from the capital to colonize the new towns and ports. North Africa and Sicily were now ruled by Carthage, and they continued improving their trade relations with the Greeks and the Italians that inhabited the Mediterranean region.

Carthage, Alexander the Great, and Agathocles

For nearly a whole century, Carthage continued its long-term plan to build and develop its trade routes and settlements, strongly focusing on trade relations and alliances. However, in the 330s BCE, a new power emerged. Alexander the Great, the leader of the new Macedonian Empire that would stretch from Greece to today's Pakistan, rose as the most important figure of the century. Stories and legends about him spread across the Mediterranean, and he was being portrayed as a god, as the new Hercules. This was cause for concern for Carthage.

The Carthaginians followed the progress of the young king, and they were afraid that he might turn his gaze to the west. Ambassadors from every nation and city-state, including Carthage, traveled to Babylon to forge friendly ties with the Macedonians. Carthage sent Hamilcar Rodanus to represent them, but he didn't go to Alexander's court to see whether he had peaceful intentions toward the Punic kingdom. He already knew that wasn't the case because, in 332, Alexander attacked the city of Tyre and enslaved its people. After the siege, the Macedonian Hercules released the Carthaginian citizens he captured during the siege and warned them that he would go to Carthage once his campaigns in Asia were finished. Therefore, Hamilcar traveled to his court to figure out when Alexander might attack Carthage.

However, we can never know what Alexander's true intentions were. Carthage was highly paranoid and afraid of being attacked by the Macedonians. So, once Hamilcar obtained information from Alexander and his court and went back to Carthage, the citizens had him executed. They believed he was a betrayer and that he must have conspired with Alexander to help him conquer the city. Not long after, in 323, Alexander passed away. He didn't get the chance to attack Carthage, and we'll never know whether he even had the plan to do so.

While Carthage could finally take a deep breath, Alexander's commanders started dividing the empire between themselves. The chaos also led to several minor nobles and ambitious officers to start carving their own fiefdoms. One of them was a young cavalry commander named Agathocles. He traveled to Syracuse and managed to instate himself as the ruler by convincing the population that all of their problems were caused by the Carthaginian dominion. Through clever manipulation and demagogy, the citizens pushed him to power.

Once Agathocles consolidated his power, he continued to study the Carthaginian military system. By doing so, he discovered a great weakness in the way a general was chosen. First of all, Carthage mostly relied on mercenary armies that were led by an elected general. This general came from Carthage, but it was the citizens of the kingdom who chose who would lead an army. This gave the general some autonomy from the elite that ruled. A general was free to make his own decisions in a military campaign, and his performance would be reviewed by the elders of Carthage. Agathocles discovered that this system created a sense of conflict between the elite and the generals. At times, a general would forget that he'd have to answer for his actions. The oligarchs who ruled Carthage were also somewhat suspicious about who was elected by the citizens. Secondly, Agathocles realized that Carthaginians weren't used to fighting wars and were therefore inexperienced on the battlefield due to their reliance on mercenaries.

Agathocles realized he could surprise Carthage by attacking them in Africa on their own soil. Their inexperience and complacency would give him the chance to attack their cities and win a great deal of plunder without bringing the war to the Sicilian cities. As a result of this move, Agathocles would gain even more support from his people. He quickly amassed all the wealth he could, and he prepared sixty ships and an army numbering 13,000 troops. His forces were small enough in number to sneak across the sea without being noticed by other ships. He landed his forces around 100 kilometers (about 62 miles) away from Carthage. As soon as he debarked, the first thing he did was set fire to the ships. He knew that he was trapped at that point, and he would have to either succeed or die trying. He used this event to sacrifice the ships to the gods and to convince his troops that they must succeed for justice and vengeance against the Carthaginians who dominated over the island of Sicily.

Carthage took notice of Agathocles's arrival, and they panicked. Two new generals were instituted to lead forces against the invader. One of them died in the first battle and lost most of his troops in a disastrous attempt to push Agathocles back. The second general retreated to the city, hoping to use this moment and take power for himself. On the island of Sicily, the Carthaginian forces that were stationed there attempted an attack on Syracuse. But they failed. Messages to Carthage reported that the army broke into several factions that fought against each other.

Carthage was on the brink of defeat, and Agathocles became more and more emboldened by his success. He also became more aggressive toward his army, and he dug deeper into his god-like complex. This caused the troops to riot against him. The fact that they hadn't been paid yet only made matters worse. Carthage noticed the situation and tried to bribe the army to abandon Agathocles. However, the Syracusan commander convinced his men to follow him into battle by making a dramatic show of committing suicide for failing them. The soldiers still respected him, so they refused the offer from Carthage.

While Agathocles was mustering his troops and waiting for reinforcements from allied Greek cities nearby, the Carthaginian general Bomilcar, who had retreated earlier, saw the opportunity to stage a coup and take over the city for himself. He ordered the respected and wealthy citizens to march into battle against Agathocles, and many of his political opponents were killed. But not long after, the younger citizens realized what was happening. They rallied themselves and moved against the tyrant. The entire city fought against Bomilcar and his soldiers, and he was defeated. The city demanded no other action besides the execution of Bomilcar. His soldiers and officers weren't punished due to the threat that lay at their gates.

Now that the rebellious general was killed, Carthage felt invigorated and more optimistic about engaging the enemy. This feeling was further bolstered when, shortly after, Agathocles received news that some cities under Syracuse's control started declaring independence. Worried by this event, he had no choice but to return to Sicily and find a solution. Although there is no mention of it, he more than likely paid for a boat to get there. He left his inexperienced son in charge of the remaining forces. With Agathocles gone, the Carthaginians became far more optimistic, and they immediately forged a new plan of action. They divided their forces into three battlegroups, each one with its own commander, and they were dispatched to take back control of different parts around Carthage that were overrun by the Syracusan forces. The new Syracusan commander made the mistake of copying the Carthaginian strategy and dividing his forces to match them. His move was unsuccessful, as

Carthage's commanders managed to outmaneuver and ambush the invading forces.

Facing defeat, the unfortunate son, Archagathus, sent a letter to his father explaining the dire situation. Agathocles resolved the matter in Sicily, and he was on his way to Carthage, but, by that point, there was no way for him to save the situation. Most of the troops were either dead or deserting. Agathocles did attempt to use the remaining forces in one more battle, but he lost. His only choice was to flee, but there was no way for him to transport the remnants of his army without risking an attack from Carthage. So, Agathocles abandoned his forces and deserted on his own. The soldiers were angry at their former commander, so they killed his son before surrendering to Carthage.

The Carthaginians struck a deal with the former troops of Agathocles to incorporate them into their own armies, then sent letters to Agathocles to find a resolution for this conflict. Both sides agreed to peace, and Carthage paid Agathocles in gold and grain to accept Carthage's legal dominion over all of his cities and territories. Dominance over Sicily was ensured once again.

The First Punic War (264– 241 BCE)

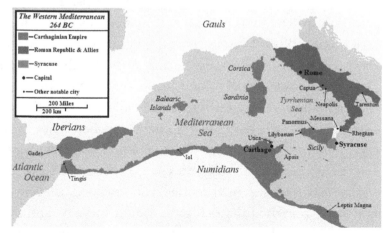

Map of the Carthaginian Empire, the Roman Republic, and Syracuse during the First Punic War

Jon Platek, CC BY-SA 3.0 <https://creativecommons.org/licenses/by-sa/3.0>, via Wikimedia Commons, https://commons.wikimedia.org/wiki/File:First_Punic_War_264_BC.png

Carthage was the undisputed economic superpower in the Mediterranean, and it was all thanks to its large, well-developed navy. A large part of their trading was done by sea, and the kingdom understood from its inception that they needed a powerful navy. Carthage brought many advancements in shipbuilding techniques, and between the 6th and 3rd centuries, their focus was placed on dominating the sea. That's why Carthage was more successful when fighting naval battles than they were at land battles. However, by the 3rd century BCE, Carthage started exerting its dominion over the other Mediterranean territories more aggressively. This worried the Romans, who were navally inferior at the time. Instead, they preferred to pay their allies for the naval transportation of troops and goods.

The last straw was when Syracuse became independent in 263 BCE, as Carthage decided to develop a new major base at Acragas. They reinforced the city and improved its harbor because the location of the city would offer them a way to eastern Sicily, which was no longer under their control. This was a threat to Roman security, so the Romans quickly sent troops to besiege Acragas. The city managed to defend itself for several months until Carthaginian reinforcements arrived, which numbered more than 55,000 troops. However, the army that was dispatched was made out of new soldiers that had never experienced real combat. Even its general, Hanno, was inexperienced. When he confronted the Romans, he made the terrible decision of placing his sixty war elephants behind his infantry. Once the Romans broke through their ranks, the untrained soldiers started running toward their line, and the panicking elephants crushed many of them. Hanno was defeated, and Acragas had to continue relying on its own defenses. The commander of the city saw no chance of surviving the siege, so he gathered his mercenaries and escaped the city. The Romans quickly breached the defenses, looted the city, and sold its citizens into slavery. Hanno survived the expedition, but he lost his citizenship and was relieved of his office.

After this major victory, the Romans realized they could press on and defeat the Carthaginian dominion in the region. They started developing their small navy quickly to offer a match for Carthage's navy. In the next four years, the Romans added over one hundred warships to their fleet, mostly consisting of quinqueremes, which were also used by the enemy. The Romans started training their new navy by organizing coastal raids. In 260 BCE, Admiral Gnaeus Cornelius Scipio was eager to add glory to his name, and he eagerly sailed to the city of Lipara, which wanted to surrender to the Roman forces. Carthage learned about the plan and sent its own naval forces to intercept the admiral. The inexperienced Roman crew quickly panicked, jumped ship, and went ashore, including their leader. Once on land, they were captured.

The Carthaginian admiral, Hannibal (still not the famous Barca), sought to find the rest of the new Roman fleet. At Messana (Messina), he encountered them, but he underestimated their numbers, and many of his ships were sunk. Rome was now even more optimistic about defeating Carthage, but the Roman consuls knew that could only be achieved by establishing naval superiority. The Romans' strength lay in disciplined hand-to-hand combat, so their engineers began modifying the ships to figure out a way to board the Carthaginian ships. They managed to do just that, and the Roman fleet sailed to hunt the enemy down.

Carthage controlled 130 ships off the coast of Sicily, and they were happy to engage the Romans, thinking they stood no chance due to their inexperience. They were wrong. The Roman soldiers grappled onto the charging enemy ships and quickly convinced the crews to surrender. Fifty ships were lost in the battle, and the rest retreated. Hannibal escaped, but he would die later in an encounter with the Roman fleets raiding the coasts of Corsica and Sardinia.

This was the point when Carthage changed its tactics. They knew from experience that they were more successful when they played the waiting game. Instead of direct conflict, they opted for a slow war of attrition. The Romans, however, weren't too happy about that because of their political system. A consul would keep his office for only a year before someone else would be elected. This system made them prefer action over long-term strategy. So, their only option was to go around Sicily and lead a military campaign in Africa.

In 256, the Romans sent a naval expedition to Northern Africa, which was a risky move because that would leave the Romans 100 kilometers (62 miles) away from any supplies or the ability to call for reinforcements. Nonetheless, Marcus Regulus took command of an armada of around 300 ships and sailed toward Africa. However, on their way there, they chose to stop in Sicily to pick up the most hardened Roman soldiers who had already fought the Carthaginians. Carthage assembled a navy to rival the Romans, consisting of around 350 ships and more than 140,000 soldiers. The naval forces clashed south of Sicily when the Romans were on their way to the African territories. This is most likely the largest naval conflict that was recorded in the ancient world.

Fortune was not on the side of Carthage during that battle. The Roman invention that allowed them to grapple onto the enemy ships proved to be an enormous advantage once again. The Roman navy divided itself into four battlegroups and charged at the Carthaginian line, breaking it. Nearly one hundred ships were captured or destroyed, while the Romans only lost around twenty. The Roman fleet then continued to Northern Africa, landing near the city of Aspis, which they quickly conquered.

Once the Roman forces established a foothold on the continent, they marched to Carthage, capturing every city, town, and settlement on their way. By the time they reached Carthage itself, the city was filled with refugees, who had flocked to the capital in search of safety from the invaders.

The war hadn't been going well for Carthage, and in the meantime, they admitted that their tactics against the Romans were flawed. To turn the tide, they recruited thousands of Greek mercenaries and an experienced Spartan general by the name of Xanthippus. By the time the Romans arrived in front of Carthage, Xanthippus was making preparations for the battle and analyzing the past battles that had been lost against the Romans. As a result, he decided to charge the Romans on the open battlefield, and through the clever use of cavalry and war elephants, he broke the Roman line, killed most of the soldiers, and managed to capture Regulus. It is assumed that the Roman commander was killed in captivity. The battle was won, but the war wasn't over, and it wasn't going well for the Carthaginians.

During the following decade, most of the battles were fought over Sicily, and hundreds of ships with tens of thousands of men were lost. While both sides suffered devastating blows, it was clear that Carthage was losing the war. Over the years, the Roman navy gathered a great deal of experience in naval warfare, and they became superior to the Carthaginians without even having to use their boarding methods. In 241, Carthage could no longer support the campaign over Sicily, as their fleet was in shambles, both due to the battles and the storms that crashed their ships into the rocky shore of Sicily. The Romans offered them their terms for peace, which included Carthage's retreat from Sicily and all the other islands between Northern Africa and Sicily. They also had to pay for war reparations and return all Roman prisoners. However, Carthage was allowed to hold onto the island of Sardinia. Carthage had no choice but to admit defeat, agree to the terms, and leave Sicily to the Romans.

The Second Punic War (218– 201 BCE)

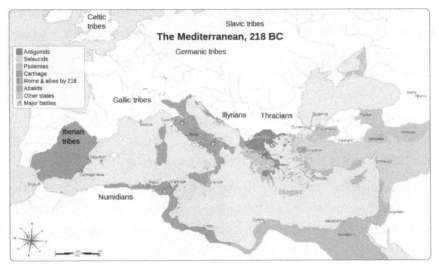

A map of the Mediterranean Basin in 218 BCE

Goran tek-en, CC BY-SA 4.0 <https://creativecommons.org/licenses/by-sa/4.0>, via Wikimedia Commons, https://commons.wikimedia.org/wiki/File:Mediterranean_at_218_BC-en.svg

After the peace treaty of 241, Carthage faced several rebellions in Northern Africa, Sardinia, and Corsica. Most of their fleet was destroyed, and these uprisings caused significant losses. The generals and governments maintaining the peace on the two islands were assassinated, and the rebels killed most of the Carthaginian soldiers as well. The Romans were watching these events unfold with great interest, and in 238, they saw the opportunity to simply take over the two islands without a fight. And they did. Roman soldiers were dispatched to Sardinia and Corsica, and they took control over them, despite being condemned for it by the Carthaginian government. However, Rome knew that Carthage didn't have the strength to oppose them after the war and after dealing with the uprisings.

The result of this situation was a new campaign into the Iberian Peninsula, which was mostly held by the natives at the time. General Hamilcar Barca was dispatched to take over Hispania and build new settlements and ports on the peninsula. He was given an army, but

Carthage no longer had enough ships to transport them over the sea. So, Hamilcar was forced to march his troops to the Strait of Gibraltar and cross there. Accompanying him was his young son, the soon-to-be-famous general Hannibal.

Hannibal was just nine years old when his father launched the conquest of Hispania, and as a result, he grew up in military camps, learning a lot from his father and the camp life. The campaign was going well against the Iberian natives, and most of the southeastern coast of Spain was quickly conquered. During these years, the power of Carthage was reinvigorated, but nine years into the expedition, Hamilcar would die, drowning during a battle under unknown circumstances. Carthage decided to continue the campaign in Hispania by electing Hasdrubal, who was Hamilcar's second-in-command and Hannibal's brother-in-law. At this point, Hannibal was already eighteen years old, and he started serving as an officer alongside Hasdrubal.

The campaign of seizing control over the Iberian Peninsula continued. However, Hasdrubal chose a different path from his predecessor. He focused on diplomacy instead of military action. He met with local tribes, established friendly relations with them, and used his wit to win them over or at least find neutral ground without shedding blood. His focus was on rebuilding Carthage's influence and honor. And he did so by consolidating his power in Hispania peacefully, at least for the most part. He also founded a new major city to solidify his position: New Carthage (today's Cartagena, Spain).

Unfortunately, his diplomatic campaign didn't last long. In 221, a slave murdered Hasdrubal, and Carthage was forced to elect a new commander to take over. Hannibal was now a twenty-six-year-old officer with experience, and he was also well respected by his men because they saw Hamilcar in him. So, Carthage chose him.

In the following two years, Hannibal began aggressively expanding his control over Hispania. He conquered several settlements and forts to the west. During this period, Hannibal proved himself on the battlefield and established himself as a clever strategist. Rome paid attention to his journey, and they became concerned about the rapid pace at which he conquered the Iberian territories. The worried Romans forged an alliance with the Iberian city of Saguntum, which was already a part of Hannibal's territories. This was his chance. Hannibal decided to go against Rome and attacked Saguntum. For more than half a year, he laid siege to the city, but eventually, he breached it.

Hannibal was also skilled in politics, and because he knew he might start a war between Carthage and Rome by this action, he sent all the sacked spoils from the city back to Carthage. The elite were thrilled, and Hannibal won their favor. However, Rome dispatched envoys to Carthage to learn whether Hannibal received orders from the state to attack their ally, Saguntum. This was a decisive moment, and the government chose to side with Hannibal. Carthage officially declared war on Rome in 218.

Once war was declared, Hannibal immediately launched his campaign against Rome. He planned to cross the Pyrenees and the Alps and attack the Romans inland. He started marching from New Carthage with an army consisting of 45,000 troops, including nearly 40 war elephants. As he crossed into Gaul, he battled several native tribes and convinced others to allow him safe passage. However, he had to leave several thousands of his men behind to hold the settlements he captured. Hannibal continued through the Alps, and against all the odds, he crossed the mountains and entered Italy with an army of 25,000 battle-hardened soldiers. Some of them perished in that journey, though we don't know the exact number, and none of his elephants survived the arduous crossing.

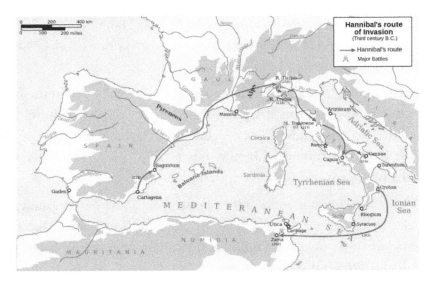

Hannibal's Campaign Route

Once in Italy, Hannibal knew that he didn't have the men to attack Rome, so he had to take control of certain provinces and secure some allies. The Romans caught up with him and engaged his forces at the Trebia River. Hannibal won the battle, and he pushed the Romans out of Lombardy. This small victory was enough to encourage the Gauls to join his campaign. Over 20,000 Gauls joined Hannibal's forces, nearly doubling his army.

Fortunately for the Romans, the winter of 217 slowed Hannibal down. This gave the Romans the chance to amass an army of 100,000 soldiers. At the same time, four legions were dispatched to defend Sardinia and Sicily. The Romans were worried that Carthage might attack them by the sea while they fought against Hannibal in the north.

As the winter passed, Hannibal continued, passing through the Chianti region. There, he faced another army of around 15,000 Romans. He defeated them without any complications, and after this, he decided to give his men a break. By that point, Hannibal's army was tired from a two-year-long campaign and from carrying the vast riches they had captured along the way. So, Hannibal decided to reach the coast and allow his men to recuperate under good weather. He also took the time to send a message to Carthage.

Carthage was happy to hear some news for the first time from Hannibal's expedition in 217, and they were overjoyed. The elders responded to their new favorite general by telling him he would receive their full support. On the other hand, while Hannibal was relaxing by the sea, Rome was gripped in terror.

As Hannibal continued south, deeper into Italy, he encountered and destroyed several small armies. By 216, the Romans realized that their tactic wasn't working. Hannibal thrived in large open battles. So, they decided to send smaller contingents, one after another, to tire the Carthaginian army. During this same year, Philip V, the king of Macedonia, offered his support to Hannibal through an alliance. However, Hannibal still did not receive any support from Carthage, despite the promises of the government. Hannibal was forced to continue fighting the Italian city-states because he didn't have the necessary strength to take on Rome directly.

For the next eight years, Hannibal didn't make much progress due to the Romans' war of attrition. Even though he defeated the Romans time and time again, and even obliterated two whole armies, he couldn't march to Rome. And Carthage still did not send him the much-needed reinforcements. The Carthaginian elite that made all of the decisions had sent their forces to maintain security over their Iberian territories. Hannibal was alone, left to recruit soldiers from Gaul and the Italian territories that had surrendered to him.

With a weakened army, Hannibal's success started to hit its end by the year 207. The Romans continued with their war of attrition, knowing that Hannibal wasn't receiving fresh troops. Furthermore, the Roman Republic allied itself with the Aetolian League to keep King Philip from joining Hannibal. Hannibal started losing in southern Italy, even though his brilliant strategies still secured some victories.

By this time, Hannibal had spent fifteen years fighting the Romans. But in 203, it was all over. Carthage recalled him home because the Romans were about to attack. Scipio Africanus had been dispatched to lead the Roman forces. Scipio was already a famous general that rivaled Hannibal's legendary skills in battle. The two admired each other, and they met to discuss the idea of a peace treaty.

There was a brief pause during 203, as the Romans negotiated with the Carthaginians to end the war. The two sides came to terms, and they weren't too unfavorable for Carthage because Rome was tired of the war. In fact, Carthage came close to agreeing to the peace settlement until the Carthaginian Senate received news that Hannibal was returning. Carthage then declined Rome's offer, feeling optimistic due to their invincible hero's return to lead them in battle.

This optimism was soon to disappear, however. In 202 BCE, Hannibal met Scipio's forces on the battlefield at Zama. The two armies rivaled each other equally, and the battle that followed was brutal. There were moments when it looked like Hannibal was winning, but Scipio was a clever tactician, and he successfully recovered from every blow. In the end, Scipio proved that Hannibal was no longer invincible. The Carthaginians lost more than 20,000 men, and almost just as many were wounded. On the other hand, due to Scipio's superior cavalry, he only suffered a little over 2,000 casualties. This defeat was a heavy blow to Hannibal and his prestige, and the people lost faith in him.

After the defeat at Zama, a peace treaty was signed, but Hannibal remained on the political scene. The Carthaginian elite chose him to be their chief magistrate, and in the following four to five years, Hannibal would demonstrate that he was also a skilled politician. He initiated several reforms in the financial area as a means of paying Carthage's debt to Rome without increasing the taxes for the people. Hannibal had determined that Carthage was capable of making the payments that were agreed upon in the treaty, but a lot of that money was being drained by corruption. A great deal of tax money never reached the state coffers because the oligarchs were stealing it. To solve the problem, Hannibal declared that the elders of Carthage were to be elected by the people and only serve for a one-year term, a move the Carthaginian citizens supported.

These reforms quickly resulted in a renewed period of prosperity. Carthage was growing again economically and stretching its influence through trade and establishing good relations with other nations. On the other hand, the oligarchs lost a great deal of fortune and status, and they became Hannibal's enemies. At the same time, Rome took notice of this renewed vigor, and they were worried that Carthage might rise again as a Mediterranean superpower. So, they dispatched a group of Roman envoys under the pretense that Hannibal was communicating with Antiochus III of the Seleucid Empire, an enemy of Rome. Hannibal knew that he stood no chance. If he waited for them to arrive, they would arrest him, as the oligarchs would surely not assist him. Hannibal's only choice was to go into voluntary exile in 195 BCE.

In the following decade, Hannibal traveled from ally to ally, from Antiochus, who resided in Ephesus, to Bithynia. All of his allies were enemies of Rome, and as an experienced general, Hannibal offered them his counsel and even led a few unsuccessful battles. He was on the run until 183 BCE, when, according to some, he met his end. It is unclear how and when Hannibal died. Some ancient Roman and Greek historians report that he died in 183, while others believe it was in 182 or 181. The method of death varies as well; some think he committed suicide or died from infected wounds. Legends say that Hannibal left a final farewell to the Romans in the form of a letter. He claimed his death would finally release the Romans from the grip of terror that he brought upon them, even as an old man in exile.

The Third Punic War and Carthage's Final Decline (149– 146 BCE)

During the decades between Hannibal's exile and the Third Punic War, the Roman Republic invested in a multitude of campaigns against the Hellenistic kingdoms in the east, as well as Hispania in the west. Rome took full control over the Iberian Peninsula, which used to belong to Carthage, as well as Sicily, Sardinia, and Corsica. In addition, several Greek and Illyrian city-states surrendered as well. Carthage was now alone, without any allies and some of their most profitable territories outside of Africa.

Furthermore, in 151, when Carthage finished paying its war indemnities to Rome, it was still bound by the treaty they had signed at the end of the Second Punic War. This treaty stated that Carthage required Rome's approval to declare war on any state or to forge an alliance. This was a problem for the Carthaginians, and their neighbors, Numidia, took full advantage of it.

The Numidians were already accustomed to raiding the Carthaginian borders due to the treaty, as they knew that Carthage couldn't declare war without Rome's approval. However, in 151, when Numidia invaded Carthage's territory, they received a different answer. Carthage saw the treaty as no longer valid because their debt to Rome had been paid. So, they amassed an army and sent it against the invader. Unfortunately for the Carthaginians, they lost the battle and had to pay Numidia the costs of their campaign. Rome was also unhappy about the situation because Carthage attacked the Numidians without their approval. Rome saw this action as a breach of their treaty.

In 149, the Roman Republic officially declared war on Carthage due to the breaking of the treaty. This new Punic war was short-lived, only lasting for three years. Carthage had significantly declined since the previous war, and they stood no chance against Rome. The Romans sailed to Carthage, capturing any settlements on their way and successfully laying siege to the city, even though they suffered some minor defeats along the way. The Carthaginians suffered through the siege for the entire duration of the war until 146, when the Roman forces under the leadership of Scipio Aemilianus breached through the defenses. The citizens of Carthage resisted, but in the end, they couldn't survive the onslaught.

Carthage was set ablaze, with many of its soldiers and citizens killed. It's estimated that around 50,000 people were taken into slavery. Rome was committed to destroying Carthage once and for all, and by 146 BCE, they were successful. Carthage's dominion was officially over, for the city was lost, and the rest of the African territories were taken under Roman rule. The once-proud Mediterranean superpower was now ashes. However, a century later, Julius Caesar would rebuild the city as the new Roman center in Africa.

Chapter 4 – The Kingdom of Aksum

The Kingdom of Aksum in the 500s

Origins

It was the location of the Kingdom of Aksum that dictated its prosperity. It was situated between various trading routes that led to Egypt, farther down in Ethiopia and to the Barbaria on the Somali coast, where valued incense was gathered. The trade advantage of this region was obvious, but it wasn't the only benefit. Aksum also faced the plains of Aksum and Hasabo, with the plateau of the Shire behind it. The position allowed the kingdom to have a very abundant rainfall season, which lasted from June to September. The soil there was fertile and crossed with many streams and freshwater springs. It is assumed that the land of Aksum was capable of producing more than one harvest per year.

However, this region was settled before the Kingdom of Aksum was founded. This is what confused early scholars, who found evidence of Sabaean influence in the region (the Sabaeans were ancient people of South Arabia). They wrongly concluded that the city of Aksum, and later the kingdom, was founded by the Sabaeans. Later discoveries proved that the influence of ancient Sabaean culture was very limited, and it even dated to the pre-Aksumite period. These new archaeological and historical discoveries put us back at the beginning. If the Sabaeans didn't set the foundation for the city of Aksum, then who did? At the moment, the question remains unanswered, and there is very little known about the formation of the Aksum state.

However, we can speculate what was going on in the site of the city of Aksum, the future capital of the kingdom. Because of its favorable position regarding trade and the fertile land that surrounded the site, it is possible that the first settlement steadily grew and developed. The population rose, as it usually happens in the areas that can sustain themselves, and with the population increase, their military strength grew too. Another possibility is that the military was used to expand the sovereignty of the city of Aksum, forging a thriving city into a kingdom. The expeditions would have been either tasked with securing the trading routes or with conquering new territories for additional resources.

It is important to understand that Aksum wasn't a foreign power coming to conquer the local peoples with their highly developed military technology. They were the locals who had managed to rise to power and subdue the surrounding peoples, using nothing else than their numbers. They might have had superior military strength due to the weapons imported from Egypt, but nothing else sets them apart as being superior in comparison to their neighbors

Besides these speculations, which are extremely sparse due to the lack of evidence, there are interesting stories and legends of the foundation of Aksum. But to understand their relevance, it is best to first describe the meaning of Aksum and its importance in the traditional history of the Ethiopians. Today, Aksum still lives, although as a little town in northern Ethiopia. But to the people, it is an ancient sacred city from which the famous Queen of Sheba ruled. It is the "second Jerusalem," where the first emperor, Menelik I, brought the Ark of the Covenant, in which the stone tablets of the Ten Commandments were kept (and still are, according to the Ethiopian Orthodox Church).

According to the Ethiopian tradition, the Queen of Sheba, or Makeda, as that is her Ethiopian name, visited Jerusalem, where she conceived with the famous king Solomon. Their son was Menelik I, to whom all the Aksumite stone obelisks and stelae are attributed. Even though the legends of Makeda, Solomon, and Menelik are still very much alive today, there are no stories and myths preserved that would give us an insight into real rulers and founders of the ancient city of Aksum. The local people love to absorb the new archaeological findings into their stories. A recently excavated mansion in the district of Dungur (near Aksum) was immediately connected to the Queen of Sheba, and it became her palace. Whether that is the actual truth is of no importance to Ethiopians, whose love for their tradition overshadows history.

But Aksum was of importance even in the stories that predate the Queen of Sheba. According to the *Book of Aksum*, a historical work from the 16th century, Ethiopia was founded by Ityopis (Ethiopis), the son of Cush, who was the son of Ham, who was the son of Noah. He built the city of Mazeber, which became the capital of the kingdom. Aksumawi, the son of Ityopis, moved the capital to the new city he founded: Aksum. Another story tells of a region of Aksum that was once ruled by a serpent king, who demanded one girl per year to be given to him as a sacrifice. In some versions of this tale, Maeda was the girl destined to be sacrificed, but a stranger named Angabo saved her, and together, they founded Aksum. All these legends were greatly influenced by Christianity, which came to Ethiopia in the 4th century CE, during the reign of King Ezana of Aksum. Some scholars believe that Christianity was the source of the legends, while others attribute them to the earlier Jewish influence, which came earlier with the various traders. However, it is generally accepted that the Christian priests used these legends to explain the connection between the Queen of Sheba, Ethiopia in general, and Solomon to the still pagan people who inhabited the region.

The Ethiopian kings continued to promote these legends. They could not have wished for a better ancient pedigree than that of the Queen of Sheba and King Solomon. They claimed descendancy from this sacred couple, who was beloved by the people, and they gained legitimacy and authority as a result. The last emperor of Ethiopia, Haile Selassie, ruled until 1974, and he even claimed to be the descendant of Menelik I, the mythical son of the Queen of Sheba and King Solomon.

Many myths and legends surround the mystical Kingdom of Aksum, but the historical evidence is very sparse. Because of it, scholars can only guess and suggest. The early governmental system of the city and kingdom is unknown. However, it can be partially reconstructed if the history of the surrounding areas is taken into account. There must have been some kind of tribal council that eventually turned into a single ruler leadership. Since the Land of Punt must have been somewhere near Aksum, it is presumed that it was them who left a system of chiefly control in Aksum's heritage. The same system was in place among the kings of South Arabia, who more than likely left their own imprint on the state of Aksum.

The city of Aksum started becoming important for its local political scene, and with the help of the military expeditions, it spread its influence to the surrounding peoples. However, there is no evidence that would suggest what relations the people of Aksum had with their neighbors, as it was only from sources of later dates that tell of Aksum's dominion over the region. Some rebellions were even described, in which the subdued peoples tried to regain their independence. But for the early period of Aksum history, the evidence that would explain their relations with other tribal people remains to be discovered.

Early Aksum

The city of Aksum was probably established somewhere at the beginning of our era, close to the 1st century CE. However, these are only assumptions based on the first written evidence about Aksum, the *Periplus of the Erythraean Sea* and *Geography* by Ptolemy, both dating from around the 1st century CE. The dating of the city was confirmed with some archaeological findings. The oldest funerary items that have been found date to the 1st and 2nd centuries. Some glass objects were later found, which radiocarbon testing showed they, too, are from around the same time. These glass objects were described in the *Periplus* as the items Aksum imported from other lands.

Greek astronomer, mathematician, and geographer Claudius Ptolemy described the city of Aksum, which was ruled by a king from his palace. Ptolemy's *Geography* was dated to 150 CE, but it is actually a revision of an older atlas. Therefore, Aksum might be of an even earlier date. However, there is no archaeological evidence that yet supports this theory. All the items excavated from the site, except for funerary and glass items, are difficult to date with radiocarbon testing, and the results are often inconclusive.

The earliest known ruler of the region was Zoskales. Although some scholars identify him as the first king of Aksum, it is quite possible that he was just a lesser tributary ruler. The exact year of his rule is not known, but it is estimated to be around the 1st century. He is mentioned in the *Periplus of the Erythraean Sea* as a ruler of Aksum, and his capital was Adulis. However, some scholars believe that his power was limited to the city and that he had no real influence over the whole Kingdom of Aksum. Adulis was a city on the shores of the Red Sea, and as such, the economy prospered there. If Zoskales was the ruler of Aksum, then the whole kingdom had already developed a strong economy and the demand for luxury goods from abroad. It is believed that during this period, the influence of the city of Aksum grew throughout the surrounding areas of Ethiopia and the coast of the Red Sea. It became the governmental center of the kingdom, and a monarchy was established.

By the time of King GDRT (thought to be Gadarat), who ruled at the beginning of the 3rd century, Aksum had grown into a political and military power capable of sending its forces across the Red Sea to fight on foreign ground. Aksum even had garrisons in the territories of Arabia, where the inscriptions that mention GDRT were first discovered. According to these inscriptions, Aksum and GDRT were allies of the king of Saba. Together, they fought against the Himyarite Kingdom (Yemen), which controlled the trade routes of the Red Sea. They crushed the Himyarite maritime control and expanded their kingdom in the Himyarite territory.

Aksum must have had a lot of power during the rule of GDRT to be able to cross the Red Sea and fight a war in foreign territory. The fact that the southern highlands of today's Yemen used to be under the control of Aksum stands as the witness of the kingdom's richness. GDRT was not only able to finance the necessary fleet for the military expedition, but he also managed to keep and further develop the conquered territories. GDRT was the first known king of Aksum who was involved in the foreign politics of South Arabia. He started the trend, which would end with a full-scale invasion of these territories in 520 when King Kaleb ruled.

The period of Aksum history from the time of the rule of King GDRT up until the beginning of the 4th century is known as the "South Arabian" period, as all the available information about the kingdom comes from South Arabian sources. Because Arabic scripture does not include vowels, the names remain known only as GDRT, ADBH, ZQRNS, and DTWNS. Historians had to add the vowels for convenience, not for historical accuracy. Therefore, GDRT might be known as Gadarat, but we cannot be sure if that was his name. ADBH is known as Adhebah or Azeba, but his name might have been completely different.

The Aksumite kings were mentioned in South Arabian inscriptions because they were part of the military campaigns that concerned their territories. Even though the inscriptions are accounts of the various wars, they do not talk about the Aksumites directly. They are concerned more with the kings of Saba and Himyar, who were, at times, the enemies of Aksum. However, from these texts, we learn that Aksum had territories in South Arabia worth fighting for. The Aksumites were also allies of both Saba and Himyar at different times and for different causes. This is evidence enough that the kings of Aksum had a political presence in South Arabia and were influential enough to change the course of the wars. Sometime between 160 and 210 CE, Gadarat allied himself with King Alhan Nahfan of Saba against Himyar. The Aksumites probably had an interest in the region because of the trade routes on the Red Sea, and they had a presence, though minor, in the region until the Persian conquest centuries later.

After the death of King Alhan Nahfan, his son and successor, Sha'ir Awtan, broke the alliance with Gadarat of Aksum. It is possible the young ruler didn't like the power Aksum was grabbing in South Arabia and saw the African kingdom as a threat rather than as an ally.

Sha'ir Awtan allied himself with the kings of Hadhramaut and Himyar, regions in South Arabia, after which the Aksumites suffered their first known loss. However, the joint forces never managed to completely expel the Aksumites from South Arabia, and so, they continued to be an influence in the region.

In 240, there was already a shift of power, and the king of Himyar allied himself with king ADBH of Aksum and his son GRMT (read as Girma, Garima, or Garmat). They fought the Sabean kings Ilsharah Yahdub and Yazzil Bayyin, who accused the Aksumites and Himyarites of breaching the peace treaty. GRMT lost the battle, but the Aksumites again continued influencing the area, meaning they were not expelled. GRMT was later mentioned again as fighting in the Aksum wars in the territory of South Arabia. At around this time, the Aksumite kings started assuming the title "king of Saba and Himyar," which might mean that they claimed suzerainty over the Arabian kings. But the inscriptions of South Arabia mention no such thing. It is possible that the title was just an attempt to proclaim dominion over the territories, but its success is unknown.

There is a big gap in the history of Aksum with no evidence to explain the course of action of the kings, their politics, or the peoples they ruled. It is presumed that it was during this time that Sembrouthes ruled, one of the most mysterious kings of Aksum. He is only known from one Greek inscription, which mentions him during his twenty-fourth year of rule. The inscription was found in Daqqi Mahari, significantly away from Aksum to the north, in today's Eritrea. The inscription doesn't say much, but it confirms him as the first known ruler to use the title "King of Kings."

The next two Aksum kings led invasions on the Himyarite Kingdom. In approximately 267/78 CE, DTWNS and ZQRNS allied themselves with al-Ma'afir and attacked Himyar. It remains unknown if DTWNS (Datawnas) and ZQRNS (Zaqarnas) were co-rulers or if they succeeded each other in a very short amount of time. Even the results of their invasion are unknown, but they did renew Aksumite involvement in South Arabian politics.

On the Ethiopian side, nothing is known of the early kings of Aksum, as the Ethiopian list of kings is of much later date. It was constructed centuries after the fall of the Kingdom of Aksum, and it deals more with the mythological hero-kings than the real ones. Often, the kings from the list do not match the historical kings, and archaeologists find it difficult to rely on traditional Ethiopian history when it comes to their work. Unfortunately, the early history of Aksum forces one to indulge in guessing and assuming, as the evidence is lacking.

From Endubis to Ezana

Endubis, who ruled approximately from 270 until 300, was the earliest known king of Aksum who issued coins. Gold, silver, and bronze coins have been discovered, and historians were able to use them to track the chronology of Aksum. The appearance of coins gives scholars a reason to believe Aksum became powerful enough to be compared to its neighbors, such as the Kingdom of Kush and Egypt. From this point on, most of what is known about the history of Aksum is through coinage, as archaeology provides us with little information. The majority of known Aksumite kings have no other archaeological evidence of their existence and would have been entirely forgotten if not for the inscriptions on the coins.

Endubis used the Roman monetary system as the base for his own. However, he used his own design for the coins, which is assumed to have been a propaganda tool. This stance is reinforced by the fact that later kings added or removed design motifs from coins as the situation in the kingdom changed. The coins also introduced a new title to the kings of Aksum, one that would remain until the 6th century, although it would reemerge later on. The title is "Bisi," and many scholars interpret it as "be'esya," which is translated from the Ge'ez language (South Semitic) as "man of...". The title was not followed by the ruler's name, but rather a name that would represent the king's tribe or a military designation.

The pagan kings of Aksum chose disk and crescent symbols for their coins. In 333 CE, King Ezana (who will be discussed a bit more below) converted to Christianity and started using a cross as his symbol. Because of this, we can differentiate Endubis, Aphilas, Wazeba, and Ousanas as pagan kings, who were all predecessors of Ezana, even though they are not mentioned anywhere else but on coins. Unfortunately, the coins of the pagan rulers can tell us little about the Kingdom of Aksum's political situation during their rules. Perhaps the only conclusion we can draw is that Wazeba and Ousanas were co-rulers at one point, as one issue of the coins combines the obverse design of Wazeba with the reverse design of Ousanas. The coins where Wazeba is represented as the sole ruler are very sparse, which leads to the conclusion that he ruled for a very short time.

All coins were issued in the Greek language, as they were used mostly for foreign trade. Even though Aksum had its own Ge'ez language, which belonged to the South Semitic group of the Ethiopian languages, Greek was commonly used to make trade easier. Only the coins of King Ezana used the Ge'ez language instead of Greek, which might suggest that during his rule, foreign trade suffered, and the import or export of goods stopped. However, this is highly unlikely, as the Kingdom of Aksum's power continued to grow. It is more probable that King Ezana tried to encourage the internal use of the coins within Ethiopia, rather than for foreign trade exclusively.

In around 270 CE, South Arabian inscriptions stop mentioning the kings of Aksum. It is possible that during the reign of King Endubis, or perhaps Aphilas, Himyar grew powerful enough to annex the Kingdom of Saba. Hadhramaut fell in around 290 CE, and the king of Himyar, Shamir Yuhar'ish, took the title of king of Saba and Hadhramaut. There is no mention of Ethiopians and their Aksumite kings. If they managed to keep some of their territories, it must have been a minor district on the coast of the Red Sea.

King Ousanas is often identified with Ella Allada, or Ella A'eda, from the traditional Ethiopian story about the Christianization of the kingdom. Although the next king, Ezana, is believed to be the one who first adopted Christianity because he started issuing coins with the symbol of the cross, Ella Allada (known by the name from his coins as Ousanas) was the first to accept the religion, at least if the traditional stories are true. The story tells of two Tyrian boys, Frumentius and Aedesius, who were traveling back from India by ship. They stopped on the coast of the Kingdom of Aksum to resupply. There, they were attacked, and while the crew of the ship was killed, the boys were spared and brought to King Ella Allada as a gift. The Aksumite king liked the boys and eventually promoted Aedesius as his personal cupbearer and Frumentius as his treasurer. Once the king died, Frumentius became a regent of the kingdom, as the king's son was still a minor. He encouraged Christian settlers to come to Aksum and build churches.

Once the king's son grew up, Aedesius and Frumentius were allowed to go to their home in Tyre. Aedesius never returned back to the kingdom, but Frumentius was later chosen to become the bishop of Aksum, and he returned and spent the rest of his life there. His task was to spread the faith through the Kingdom of Aksum, and his efforts were such that he managed to convert the young king Ezana. It might be that Ousanas never converted to Christianity, but he was sympathetic to the two boys who first brought the religion.

Ezana is the most known king of Aksum and the first who left inscriptions of his own to testify to history. He ruled approximately from 320 until 360 CE, and he was known for his many military campaigns. However, Ethiopians think that his most significant action was his acceptance of Christianity in around 333. Due to the conversion to the new faith, he had to give up on the tradition to claim his descendancy from the pagan god Mahrem.

The general belief among scholars is that the conversion of the Kingdom of Aksum to Christianity was designed to bring it closer to

Rome or Constantinople. However, Ezana was reluctant to blindly obey what these Roman cities ordered. In 356, Roman Emperor Constantius II wrote to Ezana, suggesting that he replace Frumentius as bishop and instead promote Theophilos the Indian. However, there is no evidence that Ezana bothered to reply to the Roman emperor, let alone do anything to remove his tutor and ex-regent from the position of bishop. It is possible that the Aksumite king delayed his reply on purpose, as he anticipated the death of the Roman emperor, which occurred in 361.

Ezana's titles suggest he ruled the vast areas of Yemen in addition to the whole of Ethiopia and Sudan. He used the title "King of Saba and Himyar"; however, it seems he had no actual control over the South Arabian territories. Those were just theoretical titles that suggest some sort of arrangement between Aksum and the kingdoms of present-day Yemen. Perhaps Aksum continued to control small coastal territories on the other side of the Red Sea, or maybe the titles were just traditionally inherited from his predecessors.

As for the military expeditions, for which he left detailed descriptions, Ezana mostly quelled some unrest in the surrounding kingdoms while collecting tributes. However, a major conflict was described in which the Aksum armies fought the Nubians and Kushites. The evidence of this conflict was found in both Christian Ethiopia and in pagan Meroe. While the Ethiopian inscription celebrates the victory and dedicates it to the Christian God, the one in Meroe dedicates it to the god Ares or Mahrem, which suggests that either the conflict occurred during Ezana's early reign while he was still pagan or tells of a completely different conflict that happened before Ezana's time.

The Victory Stela found in Meroe is written in Ge'ez, and as such, many historians observe it as proof that it was the Kingdom of Aksum who destroyed the Meroitic Kush Kingdom. However, others argue that the stela was a gift to the Kush because Aksum sent help to quell the Nubian rebellion. They claim that the stela did not describe the victory of Aksum over the city of Meroe but rather over the rebelling Nubians. The belief that Aksum invaded Kush and destroyed it remains unpopular because various archaeological evidence points toward economic and political instability as the main reasons for the fall of the Kushites.

From Ezana to Kaleb

The *Codex Theodosianus* suggests that contact between the Roman Empire and the Kingdom of Aksum happened often. The *Codex Theodosianus* is a compilation of Roman laws, and one of them states that anyone who traveled on official imperial business to Aksum was not allowed to stay in Alexandria for more than a year. Otherwise, he would lose the right to his imperial allowance. This law was set around the same time Constantius II sent his letter to Ezana (356). The coins issued at the beginning of the 5th century also connected the Aksumites with the Roman Empire. They are inscribed with the translation of the favorite motto of Roman Emperor Constantine: "In hoc signo vinces" ("By the sign of the cross you will conquer"). Only one Aksumite king issued such coins, and he was noted as MHDYS (Mehadeyis).

Christian mottos were often used on the coins that date from the late 4th and early 5th centuries. This is because the political climate was ripe to promote Christianity. As suggested before, the coins served a propaganda purpose, and they mirrored the political climate of the kingdom. All the kings after Ezana, at least those whose coins offer archaeological evidence, believed in the Christian faith, and as such, they became the saints of the Ethiopian Orthodox Tewahedo Church. Although both Ezana and his brother, Saizana, are revered as saints today, the Ethiopian tradition refers to them as Abreha and Asbeha. Scholars today believe that these were the baptismal names of the royal brothers.

As Christianity spread through the Kingdom of Aksum, the funerary customs changed. The last and largest funerary stelae were dated to the late 4th or early 5th century. The monolithic monument fell very soon after it was made, probably during the reign of King Ouazebas, whose coins were found beneath it.

The first sign of the decline of the Kingdom of Aksum may have been found in a letter written by a man named Palladius. It is possible, but not certain, that he was a bishop of Helenopolis who lived from 368 until 431. His task was to travel to India and send a report on Brahmin philosophy, but to whom the letter was addressed remains unknown. In the letter, he tells the story of an Egyptian lawyer who stayed in Aksum on his way to India. Palladius refers to the king of Aksum as *basilikos micros*, a title that could be interpreted as "a minor kinglet." However, scholars still discuss how to properly interpret the word *basilikos*, as it seems that, in some instances, it is attributed to people of great importance, especially when it came to Nubian rulers. Whatever *basilikos* means, the attribute *micros* attached to it is certainly unflattering.

Next to Ezana, the best documented king of Aksum was Kaleb. His Ge'ez inscription is **KLB 'L SBH WLD TZN**, and he is the first king for whom an inscription with vowels was found; therefore, we know his full name was Kaleb 'Ella Asbeha, son of Tazena. Kaleb, probably a variation of the biblical name Caleb, was his birth name, but he is also known by his royal name, 'Ella Asbeha, and its Greek varieties, Hellesthaeus or Ellestheaeus. Unfortunately, as with the other kings of Aksum, the dates of his life are not preserved, but the general conclusion that historians make is that he was born around 510, ruled around 520, and died somewhere around 540.

Since Aksumite kings often used several names, it remains yet to be discovered who Kaleb referred to when he says he is the son of Tazena. No evidence sheds light on that name, as no king ruled under that name. It is possible that Kaleb was talking about some older ancestor who predated coinage. Maybe it was important for him to put an emphasis on the connection between him and the royal dynasty to prove the legitimacy of his rule.

Other theories try to find the appropriate ruler who could be Kaleb's father. It is quite possible that one of the previous Aksumite kings used Tazena as his royal name, but he went by some other name, perhaps his birth name. From the numismatic point of view, the obvious choice would be King Ousanas, whose coins predate Kaleb's. Aside from Kaleb's coins that describe him as the son of Tazena, this name is mentioned in the traditional Ethiopian list of kings. However, that list was written centuries after the fall of the Kingdom of Aksum, and it often doesn't match the archaeological findings. This doesn't mean it should be completely ignored, though.

Besides the coinage, information about Kaleb's rule can be found in various texts. In 1920, a book written in the classical Syriac language was found in Yemen. The pages of the book were used as a padding for the cover of a 15th-century book. Fortunately, scholars managed to reconstruct around fifty-two pages, and they named it the *Book of the Himyarites.* It was written at the beginning of the 5th century, but the preserved pages were from a copy, which the author signed himself and added a date when he finished the work: April 10th, 932. The *Book of the Himyarites* must have been an extensive work because the list of chapters numbers forty-two. Much of the book was destroyed, but the part that is of interest to the history of Aksum was preserved in fragments. The text mentions a war in Himyar that was fought between Kaleb and Jewish King Yusuf Asar Yathar (also known as Dhu Nuwas). There is also mention of another Aksumite expedition to Himyar led by someone named Hiuna. However, scholars are unable to connect this name to any known Aksumite king. It is possible that he ruled before the coins were first issued throughout the kingdom. There is a theory that connects him to King Kaleb, in which case Hiuna would be a military general. In one of his own inscriptions, Kaleb writes how he sent HYN (possibly Hiuna) BN ZSMR with troops to found a church in Himyar.

From the *Book of the Himyarites*, we learn that Kaleb fought the Jewish king in 520, who had persecuted the Christians of Himyar.

Kaleb defeated and killed King Yusuf, and in his place, he appointed a Christian named Sumuafa Ashawa, who was a native of Najran, where most of the Christians were persecuted. Because of the sheer number of sources available that speak of these and other events of Kaleb's reign, Kaleb is often regarded as the most important Aksumite king. However, many of these sources are of later date, and they repeatedly celebrate Kaleb's actions to preserve Christianity. His actions in Himyar alone earned him a place among the Ethiopian saints. He was even listed among the Roman martyrs, even though he belonged to Oriental Orthodoxy, which is considered heresy by the Roman Catholic Church.

Even though all the sources celebrate Kaleb for his defense of Christianity, the true purpose of his invasion of Yemen might be more political. Some of the sources mention that Himyar had belonged to Aksum before the Jewish king managed to take it over when the Aksumite appointee to the throne died. It was winter at the time, and the Aksumites couldn't cross the Red Sea to defend their territories in Arabia. If Kaleb allowed Yusuf to keep the throne, not only would the Christians suffer persecution, but the Jewish king would also have access to all the trade routes of the Red Sea, and he would have become a source of great competition to the economy of Aksum.

After Kaleb's viceroy Sumuafa Ashawa died in 525, an Aksumite general named Abraha proclaimed himself a king. He had probably plotted to dispose of the native viceroy, and for this, Kaleb sent an army of 3,000 men to punish Abraha and his supporters. However, the army defected. They killed their leader and joined Abraha instead. Infuriated, Kaleb sent another army, but he just couldn't win against Abraha. Finally, he was forced to leave him alone to rule as the king of Himyar. For unknown reasons, Kaleb abdicated the throne, sent his crown to Jerusalem to be displayed in the Holy Sepulchre, and then retired to a monastery.

Kaleb's son now ruled. He is known by the name W'ZB (Wa'zeb), and he added "son of Ella Atsbeha" to his name, which was a variation of his father's royal name. However, nothing else is known about him. The coins that date from his rule are all inconclusive, as they bear different names. These coins were also of lesser quality, which is usually attributed to the economic decline of the Kingdom of Aksum. This decline had begun during the reign of King Kaleb. The wars across the Red Sea cost Aksum too much money and manpower, and thus, the decline of the kingdom started in the mid-6th century.

It is possible that the Plague of Justinian (541–549) reached the Kingdom of Aksum, although some sources claim it started in Ethiopia. The Aksumites used the term "Ethiopia" since the 4th century for territories beyond their kingdom, and it remains unclear if the sources meant Aksum or other parts of Africa when mentioning Ethiopia. If the plague reached Aksum, it could explain why Kaleb and his successors were unable to control or dispose of King Abraha in Yemen.

When the son of Abraha inherited the throne of Himyar, he resumed his allegiance to the Kingdom of Aksum and paid tribute to its king. However, his brother, Ma'd-Karib, rebelled and asked Justinian the Great, the Eastern Roman emperor, for help. When he declined, Ma'd-Karib turned to Khosrow I, the Sasanian emperor of Persia. He sent 800 men to help Ma'd-Karib, although different sources mention different numbers. By some, the Persian army numbered 3,600, while others say 7,500. The truth is elusive, but modern estimations go even higher, mentioning over 16,000 souls. The Aksumite-Persian war took place completely in the territories of Arabia, with Masruq, another son of Abraha, leading the Aksumite armies as their viceroy. Masruq died in battle, and the Aksumites were defeated. The Persians conquered Yemen and wrestled it out of Aksumite hands. However, somewhere between 575 and 578, the Aksumites returned and tried to take their precious possessions back. Persia sent another army and managed to expel the Aksumites from

Arabia, and they never returned. Yemen remained in Persia's hands until the 7th century.

The Decline of the Kingdom

There are many factors that influenced the decline of the Kingdom of Aksum, as well as many theories and conclusions about it. The evidence provides some insight on what happened around the city of Aksum. Besides the wars in Yemen, which were very costly, the economy of the kingdom was greatly influenced by the land around the city of Aksum. Up until that point, the land was fertile and able to feed the population. However, climatic evidence suggests that there was not enough rain in the region throughout the beginning of the 7th century. More money was spent on importing food, and local production slowed to a halt. During the late 7th century and the beginning of the 8th century, the people of Aksum were forced to exploit the land as much as they could, which only fastened its degradation. Eventually, the once-fertile lands of Aksum had to be abandoned, and the people retreated to the south.

At the same time, the territories Aksum held on the coast of the Red Sea were lost to the Rashidun Caliphate. The people sought protection in the southern highlands, abandoning the city of Aksum as their capital. The expansion of Islam saw to it that the name Aksum was no longer applied to the Ethiopian people. Although Arabic sources still referred to Aksum as the great and rich kingdom, they called it by a different name: "Habashat." At around the same time, during the 7th century, the Kingdom of Aksum completely stopped issuing coins. Due to the rapidly declining economy, they had become obsolete. Instead, cloth and salt were used for bartering, and it seems that all the trade Aksumites performed during this period were limited to the neighboring countries in Africa and Arabia.

The Kingdom of Aksum started gaining some territories in the south, but that did not bring back the economic power or the old glory the kingdom once held. By losing the coast of the Red Sea, Aksum became economically isolated, doomed to a steady decline.

Also, all the relations Aksum had with the outside world was with Islamic states, and as a Christian kingdom, this made the isolation even worse. Ethiopian bishops were still appointed from Alexandria, but even Egypt was now a Muslim state, and all the appointments had to be approved by a Muslim governor.

When the city of Aksum was abandoned, new capitals started emerging. However, the sources are not consistent. Arabic authors wrote about Jarmi or Jarma and Ku'bar or Ka'bar. These cities were mentioned in the 9th century, but astronomer Al-Battani, who was from the 10th century, mentions the city of Aksum, albeit with the slightly changed name of "'Ksumi." It is possible that the city of Aksum still existed but had been reduced to a simple town or settlement. It was no longer a capital, as in 833, another Muslim astronomer mentioned Jarma as the capital of the kingdom of Habash (Aksum). The city continued to be mentioned in various Arabic sources throughout the 9th and 10th centuries as the city of the Habasha kings. Ku'bar was mentioned at around the same time as being the capital of the Habash kingdom, but it remains to be known if it was a different city or simply Jarmi under another name. These cities are lost to history.

The traditional Ethiopian history includes the story of Jewish Queen Gudit, to whom they prescribe the destruction of the Kingdom of Aksum. According to legend, she ordered the destruction of Aksum's churches, cities, and countryside. She also burned books, artwork, and anything that would display the previous ruling dynasty. She was determined to put the dynasty of Aksum to an end. However, the tale of Gudit and the destruction of Aksum is preserved only in oral history. Any written material on the subject is just a transcription of that oral story, which was passed down through the years.

However, there is evidence of the burning of churches in around 960, which would correspond to the Gudit period, if she even existed. However, there is no evidence of a Jewish queen's presence in Aksum whatsoever. Although there is evidence that a female ruler ruled

Aksum in the 10th century, it is more probable that it was the pagan Queen Bani al-Hamwiyah, who would have invaded the region from the south.

The Aksumite Kingdom continued to exist throughout the 12th century under the new the Zagwe Dynasty. But the kingdom was already very weak, and it held only a fraction of the territory it once possessed. The last Zagwe king was killed by Yekuno Amlak, the founder of the Solomonic Dynasty, which lasted until 1974. The Kingdom of Aksum was officially over, and in its stead was the new Ethiopian Empire. However, the Aksumite culture continued to live through its descendants. The people remained the same, no matter which kingdom or empire they belonged to, and the Aksumite influence in the architecture and art of Ethiopia is still recognizable today.

Chapter 5 – The Ghana Empire

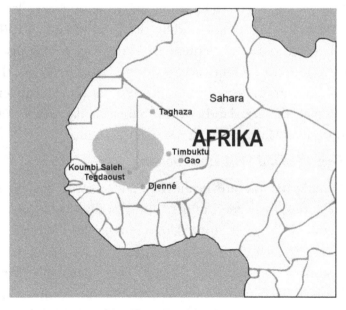

A representation of the Ghana Empire at its peak, colored in green

Luxo, CC BY-SA 3.0 <http://creativecommons.org/licenses/by-sa/3.0/>, via Wikimedia Commons, https://commons.wikimedia.org/wiki/File:Ghana_empire_map.png

Today's Ghana is territorially different from the ancient kingdom or medieval empire of Ghana. The country we know today was named after the empire, or, rather, it was named after their title for a ruler. The name of the empire was actually Wagadu (Wagadou), and it was ruled by a king whose official title was "Ghana." Scholars cannot agree on when the Ghana Empire was founded. There is archaeological evidence of a settlement that dates before the year 300 CE. However, that settlement belonged to the Dhar Tichitt culture, which abandoned the area, probably pushing southward due to the invading nomadic tribes. The nomadic tribes who settled in the area between the year 300 and 500 belonged to the Soninke people, and it was they who named the area Wagadu.

But if modern Ghana has nothing to do with the ancient empire, where exactly was it? Fortunately, it is possible to pinpoint the location due to various written sources left by the Arabs who settled in Morocco and Sudan during the 7th century. Another great source of information comes from archaeology, which came very late to the region. In fact, the first major finding occurred as late as 1969 when Dhar Tichitt, the oldest settlement in West Africa, was discovered. The Ghana Empire had no access to the Atlantic coast. It was a landlocked area around one hundred miles north of the River Niger, and it occupied the grasslands of the Sahel. Today, these territories belong to western Mali and southeastern Mauritania.

The Legend of the Wagadu Kingdom

The Soninke people are proud of their storytellers, and through music and stories, the legend of their kingdom has been passed down from generation to generation. Although the stories have changed through time, as each generation adds its own details or forgets old ones, the story of the origins of Wagadu is essentially the same. The oral tradition of the Soninke people talks about a common ancestor, Dinga, who came to Ghana from somewhere in the Middle East.

Dinga settled in a town named Dia, located in the Niger Delta. He married and had two sons, who moved to different towns in the Sahel grasslands and became the forefathers of the Soninke people. Both Dinga and his sons often moved from one place to another. This is a part of the legend that explains why the Soninke people are found in various parts of the Sahel. Eventually, Dinga arrived at a place in today's Mali, southwest of the modern-day town of Nioro du Sahel. This land was inhabited by spirits at that time, with whom Dinga fought a magical battle. After he defeated all the spirits, he married their daughters and had many sons, who became the leaders of many Soninke clans. The Cisse clan eventually became the ruling dynasty of Wagadu.

The legend continues and tells of Dinga as an old and blind man who had to decide who of his sons was worthy of becoming chieftain after his death. After he decided to proclaim his oldest son as his successor, the youngest, named Diabe Cisse, disguised himself as his elder brother and tricked Dinga into giving him all his chiefly powers. But after Dinga's death, Diabe Cisse had to run from his brother's wrath, and he hid in the wilderness. There, he found a magical drum, which, if beaten, summoned four cavalry commanders from four sides of the world. They recognized Diabe Cisse as their leader and became chiefs of the four provinces once the Wagadu Kingdom was founded.

Now that he had followers, Diabe Cisse needed a place to settle. He found a perfect location at the site of what would become Koumbi Saleh, the capital of the Ghana Empire. But this site was guarded by a giant python. The young chief made a deal with the snake that he could settle in the area if the python, named Bida, remained its guardian. However, Bida demanded one beautiful girl to be given to him as a sacrifice each year. In return, the snake guaranteed plenty of rain to fall in the region, making the ground quite fertile.

Thus, the Kingdom of Wagadu was founded. The four commanders of Diabe Cisse became the aristocratic clans, called *wago*, and it was them who gave the name to the kingdom, as Wagadu is a shortened version of its original name *wagadugu* —"the land of wago." There also may have been some truth to the story of a girl being sacrificed. The legend continues, claiming that each year, a different province had to provide the girl. This practice might have been set in place to promote the unity of the provinces and their chieftains.

Later generations added their own stories into the legend of Wagadu. One of them tells the story of the kingdom's decline through an allegory. Many generations later, a young girl, who was chosen to be sacrificed to Bida, was engaged to an aristocrat. Angered, the young man jumped in front of the python and cut off his head. While dying, Bida cursed the kingdom with a drought and a lack of gold. The Soninke people were forced to abandon their capital and find their luck elsewhere. Four provinces, which were led by different clans, broke the ties that bound them into one kingdom. The story of the curse symbolizes the climate change that occurred in the Sahel. The rain stopped, making the ground dry and impossible to work. The climatic change may have led to the gradual decline of the Wagadu Kingdom. By the 13th century, the kingdom ceased to exist at all.

Trade

The Soninke people started trading with other Berber peoples of the Sahara region. In fact, they used these Saharan nomadic tribes as their intermediaries in trade with the African regions north of the Sahara Desert. This trade allowed the Ghana Empire to emerge as one of the richest kingdoms of Western Africa. They also controlled a source of gold, which did not come from the mines but was rather washed down from the highlands by excessive rain. It was simply collected from the streams that had been created by the rains. This is another reason for the downfall of the Ghana Empire, as the climate change meant less rain, and, in turn, gold did not flow to the region anymore.

The king of Ghana was one of the wealthiest kings of Africa because he took all the gold nuggets for himself, allowing the people who collected it to keep only gold dust. Another reason for his wealth was the trade tax he imposed on salt. Everyone who imported salt had to pay one gold coin, but those who exported it had to pay two gold coins. The early trade with the Berbers of the Sahara brought horses and iron to the Soninke of Ghana. The weapons they crafted and the implementation of horseback warfare brought Ghana dominion over the other smaller clans. The imported iron was also used to make tools for working the land. Its fertile ground attracted more people to the capital of Wagadu, Koumbi Saleh. In turn, the city grew into an important trading outpost.

It was this developed trade across the Sahara Desert and the subjugation of the neighboring clans that elevated the status of Ghana from a kingdom to an empire. With the people of the Sahara, the Soninke traded copper, dates, and salt. But they also exported the products of their savanna regions, such as slaves, iron tools, weapons and utensils, livestock, hides, cloth, clay pottery, medicinal herbs, food (especially various grains), spices, fruit, and honey. One of the main export items of Ghana was kola nuts, which are rich in caffeine and were used as a way to quickly state hunger and reenergize the tired nomadic people. Kola nuts are still used in Western Africa as a symbol of hospitality, but in the 1800s, they were exported to the United States, where they were used as a sacred flavoring ingredient of Coca-Cola.

The position of the Kingdom of Ghana allowed it to control and dominate the Sahara routes used by the trade caravans. These elaborate paths through the desert took the products and gold from Ghana to the distant regions of the Middle East and the Mediterranean Sea. From there, they easily found their way to the various ships that sailed around the known world. By the 5th century, camels were introduced to the north of Africa, and they became a widely used animal for transport over the Sahara Desert. This animal was responsible for the quick development of trade in Western Africa. The trade caravans consisted of anywhere between 6 to 2,000 camels, which would carry the huge load without the need for water or food for many days.

The travel on the Saharan trade routes lasted two or three months, and expert guides of the Sanhaja Berber people were needed. They lived nomadic lives in the Sahara and knew all the places where food and water were available. Without them, a trade caravan was doomed to disappear in the harsh environments of the desert.

But the Ghana Empire did not control only the trade across the Sahara. Its unique position and growing economic power allowed it to control the trade in the south too. There, the savanna and forest regions, which were rich with resources, offered their goods for the taking. Ghana also imported northern products to the south, such as glass, iron tools, silk, porcelain, jewelry, perfumes, spice, and sugar. Ghana also had easy access to the north and northwest of Africa. Those trade routes connected the kingdom with Maghrib, Egypt, and Tripoli. Because of its convenient location, Ghana was the meeting point for many merchants traveling across Africa. And the king collected taxes from all of them, making himself ever richer.

The Cities

Koumbi Saleh has been described as the capital city of the Ghana Empire. However, the sources that mention this city are often contradictory. The area where the city was founded was inhabited from earlier times, as we saw in the Wagadu legend, but it remains uncertain if it was indeed the capital. The earliest written mention of the city is from the 8th century when one of the Persian astronomers mentions it in his writing about the Ghana Empire. It was the early medieval Arab writers who mistook the title Ghana for the name of the land, and as a result, it is still remembered as Ghana to this day.

The great Muslim geographer and historian, Al-Bakri, was the first to describe Koumbi Saleh in detail. He lived in Andalusia in the 11th century, and although he never stepped on African soil himself, he collected the information from various merchants and travelers. Because the medieval world was dominated by fantastical stories instead of pure facts, Al-Bakri's writing is filled with mistakes. Nevertheless, it offers insight into the life of the city and its significance for foreign trade. One of the first mistakes he made was to identify the name of the city with the name of the land. Therefore, he thought that the capital of Ghana was also called Ghana. But due to his insistence on calling it the capital, scholars have concluded that he was writing about Koumbi Saleh.

Al-Bakri describes the capital of Ghana as two very close cities that were ten kilometers (six miles) apart. One was the king's city, which was inhabited by the pagans. The other one was a Muslim city that had twelve mosques. In between the two cities, the commoners lived in a row of huts and houses. This would mean that the two cities were connected. Al-Bakri claimed that the Muslim city was named El-Ghaba, while the king's city was Ghana.

The first archaeological evidence of Koumbi Saleh was excavated in 1914 by a French team of archaeologists. The ruins were found in the Sahel region of today's south Mauritania. The ruins were dated anywhere from the 9th century to the 14th century, and one mosque was discovered. There are no links that would identify these ruins with anything Al-Bakri described, and the second city was never discovered in the vicinity. However, the size of the city is crucial. Modern estimates believe it could have held around 20,000 people. For this region, that number signifies an important city. If Koumbi Saleh wasn't the capital of the Ghana Empire, it certainly was one of the most important trade hubs. The lack of evidence that would connect the excavated ruins with the capital described by Arabic sources makes some historians believe that Koumbi Saleh wasn't Ghana's capital at all.

But the oral tradition of the Soninke people still claims that the capital of their kingdom was "Kumbi," or Koumbi, Saleh. Al-Bakri might have been told by others that the capital of Ghana was made of two cities, but in the past, it was common for Muslims to have separate districts. It is possible that this was the case with Ghana's capital and that the Muslim geographer simply misunderstood the stories. Archaeologists have found two sections of Koumbi Saleh, but they are not six miles apart as Al-Bakir claimed.

Another very important trade city was discovered 125 miles northwest of Koumbi Saleh. It is the city named Awdaghust, which was probably founded during the golden age of the Ghana Empire in the late 10th or early 11th century. Al-Bakri wrote about this city as well, describing it as large, crowded, and well built. It was built in the shadow of a barren mountain, and it prospered because it was an oasis town on the trans-Saharan trade route. Its population was mostly Muslim traders from North Africa, but there were also some local peoples, probably of Berber descent. They were farmers who grew wheat, dates, fig trees, and henna (a plant from which red dye is produced).

Islam and the Decline of the Ghana Empire

Islam spread to the Berber people of the Sahara region during the 8th century. It came from Morocco and other Northern African states where the Umayyad Dynasty had spread its influence. However, the sub-Saharan territories converted almost two centuries later, during the reign of the Almoravid Dynasty. During the beginning of the 10th century, the Almoravids were at the peak of their power, but the Sanhaja peoples were slow to convert. The clan chiefs were the first to accept the new religion, but Islam was generally much weaker in Western Africa due to its distance from Islam's epicenter in Mecca.

Around 1042, the Almoravid movement started gaining momentum and took over the Berber tribes of the Sahara. Their prime concern was the weakness of Islam in Africa, and they devoted their lives to teaching the strict rules of the religion. They wanted African followers to read the Quran, to stop drinking any alcoholic drinks, and to start fasting and praying several times a day. To spread the movement across Africa, they needed to unite the clans of the southern Saharan Sanhaja people. The tribes joined the political federation of the Almoravid movement so quickly that, by 1048, the army they had gathered was strong enough to challenge their neighbors. By 1054, the Soninke of the Ghana Empire lost Awdaghust, but the federation didn't linger there. Instead, they crossed the Sahara and reached southern Morocco.

However, the influence of the Almoravids continued to press the Soninke people of Ghana, and they had no other choice but to abandon their old religion, which worshiped snakes, and join Islam. The decline of the kingdom did not occur with the arrival of the Almoravid movement, though. Instead, Ghana was determined to save its position as a powerful economic force. They managed to retrieve Awdaghust and continued to control the trade routes of the Sahara Desert. The archaeological evidence in both Awdaghust and Koumbi Saleh confirms that Ghana remained very rich and powerful until at least the 12th century.

But the struggle continued. The Sanhaja people were determined to wrestle the control of trade from Ghana's grip. The constant attacks were followed by the climatic change, which pressured the Soninke people to abandon their once-prosperous cities and search for more fertile lands. In the 12th century, the decline of Ghana was rapid, and it left a power vacuum in Western Africa. Gradually, the small chiefdoms of the savanna started uniting and formed small kingdoms around the rivers and lakes that were still rich with rainfall, such as the Upper Niger. During the 13th century, the small kingdoms united to form a state, one that would become known as the Mali Empire.

Chapter 6 – The Mali Empire

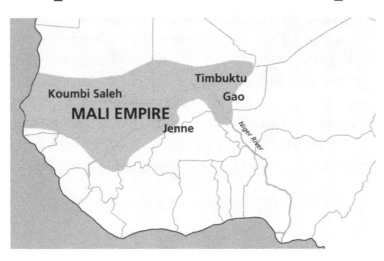

The Mali Empire at its height, including the location of Timbuktu

While Ghana was declining, the Soninke people, who migrated to escape the dry, infertile areas, were assimilated into the numerous small kingdoms that started to form across the savanna. To the south of Ghana, the Kaniaga (the Susu kingdom), Mema, and Diara kingdoms rose to power on the banks of the River Niger and its tributaries. The lands there were still fertile and could sustain all the

---

newcomers. Some of these kingdoms were already Muslim, but most of them continued the traditional practice of polytheistic religions.

The most powerful among the polytheistic kingdoms was Susu (Sosso). Its ruling family was named Kante, and they were blacksmiths. In the small society of the kingdom, the blacksmiths enjoyed high status, as they were the ones with the power to command fire to subdue iron and bend it into the tools that served the whole community. Because of the almost magical powers of blacksmiths, they were also chosen to be the religious leaders of the clans.

The Susu kingdom was centered around the region today known as Beledougou. This territory lay north of Bamako, the capital of today's Republic of Mali. Unfortunately, no archaeological excavations were performed in the region, and the only source about the Susu kingdom we have comes from the writings of the Arab scholars who traveled the region as they followed the trade caravans. The oral tradition of the locals still identifies them as the Susu community, and one of the nearby villages still bears the name Susu.

In the 12th century, Susu took over some of the territories that used to belong to the Ghana Empire. Information about this traveled to Cairo, where Ibn Khaldun, an Arab scholar, interviewed many traders who came from the Mali Empire. He wanted to write down the history of the people of West Africa, and he listened to the stories of those who came to Egypt to trade. They told him that Susu was the greatest and most powerful kingdom in the region and that it was ruled by King Sumanguru Kante. The merchants had many fantastical stories about their king, who, according to them, was a great conqueror and sorcerer. The first kingdoms he conquered lay just to the south of Susu, on both banks of the Niger. They were independent Mande chiefdoms that shared culture and trade.

The Mande chiefdoms had ruled their lands as subject kings of the Ghana Empire during the 11th century. With the dissolvement of the Ghana Empire, they gained their independence, and they wouldn't allow Susu to take over what Ghana had left. Instead, they chose to rebel and free themselves of the Susu kingdom. Here, the epic oral tale of Sunjata tells its version of the foundation of the Mali Empire. The Sunjata epic is still told among the Mande people of Mali, and it has many variations, as each region tells its own version of the epic. However, they all agree that a certain hero, named Sogolon Sunjata, managed to overthrow Susu King Sumanguru Kante and start what would become known as the Mali Empire.

In some versions of the epic, the hero's name is Sundiata of the Keita clan. He was born as a cripple and couldn't walk throughout his childhood. After his father's death, his brother took over the rule of the kingdom, exiling Sundiata Keita and his mother. No neighboring kingdom would shelter the pair, and they traveled to the distant land of Mema. There, he grew to be a famous warrior. Some versions of the story even mention that he was so popular that he was chosen to inherit the throne of Mema. However, when Sundiata heard of the troubles the Mande kingdom had with the Susa and its evil sorcerer-king, he decided to go back and free his people. He managed to unite the peoples of the neighboring kingdoms and combine the armies of Wagadu, Mema, and Mande to defeat the Susu kingdom. At the Battle of Kirina, in the Koulikoro region (today's Mali), Sumanguru Kante was killed, and Sundiata Keita destroyed the Susu. Arabic sources date this battle to 1235, which is often used as the year when the Mali Empire was founded.

From Sunjata to Sakura

Information about the Mali Empire mostly comes from the Arab historians, scholars, and explorers, such as Shihab al-Din al-Umari (1300–1384), Ibn Battuta (1304–1369), and Ibn Khaldun (1332–1406). They traveled the medieval Islamic world and collected the stories of the rise and fall of the empires of Africa. According to them, Sunjata ruled for twenty-five years after he founded the Mali Empire and the Keita Dynasty. He was the first to be granted the title Mansa, which comes from the Mandinka word for a king or emperor. After his death, he was succeeded by his son, Mansa Wali, known to the

Arab world as Mansa Ali. He was the only biological son of the hero Sunjata and the first king of Mali to convert to Islam. His adoptive brothers and successors, Wati and Khalifa, were the sons of Sunjata's brother.

Oral tradition tells the story of Mansa Wali being too young to inherit the throne after his father. His uncle was supposed to rule, but the young prince was too ambitious, and he took the throne by force. However, he had no sons of his own to inherit after him, leaving the kingdom to his uncle's sons. During his rule, Mansa Wali made the pilgrimage to Mecca somewhere between 1260 and 1277. Wali is remembered as a king who excessively worked on expanding the territories of the Mali Empire to the west of Africa, as well as for bringing reforms to agriculture, economy, and politics.

Unfortunately, he was succeeded by his adopted brothers, who brought nothing to the empire. The first to rule after Mansa Wali was Wati. However, there is no memory of his kingship in either oral tradition or in the written sources of Arab scholars. This leads one to conclude that he did nothing for the empire. The next to rule was the other brother, Khalifa. He is remembered but for all the bad reasons. Khalifa was an insane king who liked to practice archery by shooting at his people. Eventually, an angry mob killed him.

It is unknown whether the two brothers who inherited after Mansa Wali had sons, but the next ruler was the son of Sunjata's sister, Abu Bakr. This is a tradition that was possibly adopted from the remnants of the Ghana Empire, as their succession was matrilineal. However, it seems that the dynastical struggles continued for the Mali Empire, as the next ruler was a military commander, not a member of the royal family. Sakura, who ruled from 1298 until 1308, grabbed the throne, probably with the support of the people. He also made a pilgrimage to Mecca, which is proof that he had the support of his people. Otherwise, it would have been very unwise for him to leave the empire at such a sensitive time.

Sakura was one of the best kings the Mali Empire had. He made Mali into a powerful empire that controlled the trade to the north of Africa, a role Ghana once had. New economic growth was acquired, and Mali prospered as a result. Feeling confident in his empire, Sakura embarked on a series of military expeditions that expanded the territories of Mali. The most significant conquest was probably the city of Gao. Located on the eastern bank of the Niger River, this city proved to be one of the most important trade hubs of the trans-Saharan routes. The city was rich and already under Muslim rule, so the transition to becoming a part of Mali went smoothly.

Sakura died on his way back to Mali after his pilgrimage. For some unknown reason, the empire reversed to the previous dynasty of Sunjata's descendants. Several more insignificant kings ruled the Mali Empire until it finally passed to the famous Mansa Musa in 1312, the greatest and richest ruler of West Africa.

Mansa Musa and the City of Timbuktu

Mansa Musa of the Keita clan ruled the Mali Empire for twenty-five years (1312–1337). His reign is considered to be the golden age for the people of Mali. He was a very pious and generous king, and according to the Arab historian Ibn Kathir, he was a young man when he inherited the throne, which ruled over twenty-four lesser kingdoms.

However, Mansa Musa did not inherit the throne once his predecessor died. Instead, he was chosen as a regent of the empire when Mansa Abu Bakr II went on a controversial journey across the Atlantic Ocean. The story, which was written down by Arab scholars, tells about Abu Bakr's insatiable curiosity about what lay at the end of the Atlantic Ocean. He sent an expedition to see what was beyond the great water, but only one boat came back. The rest sank, probably in a storm. Unsatisfied, the king set sail himself, preparing 2,000 boats to hold the men and 1,000 for food and water. None of the people who went across the ocean with Abu Bakr ever returned, and to this day, it remains a mystery if they ever reached the New World.

Once it was obvious Abu Bakr II was not coming back from his travels, Musa Keita was elevated from regent to king, gaining the title of mansa in the process. Described as a great man by Arab sources, Mansa Musa sat on a throne completely made out of ebony, ornamented with huge elephant tusks. Both the king and his officials wielded weapons purely made out of gold when meeting the representatives of other kingdoms. Mansa Musa had around thirty slaves constantly at his disposal, serving him and his companions. One of the slaves was always tasked with holding a sunshade made out of silk over the king's head. The shade had a falcon ornament at the top, made out of pure gold.

Other descriptions of the Mali king mention music accompanying him whenever he went out in public. He never talked or gave speeches in public. Anything he had to say was whispered to his chief spokesmen, who would then make public announcements for him. Two horses always followed the king's procession. They were a sign of wealth, as they were the most expensive animals in Western Africa, but they weren't just for showing off. They were fully equipped and ready in case the mansa had to ride them.

It wasn't unusual for southern African rulers to go to Mecca on a pilgrimage (known as the Hajj), but he was certainly the most famous one. As a devout Muslim, Musa did not impose his religion on the common people of the Mali Empire, but he did make it an obligatory religion for the aristocracy. Even though some of the people he ruled were still pagans, the Muslim religious holidays were celebrated around the empire as national sacred days. During his rule, Islam prospered in sub-Saharan Africa, and many kingdoms converted willingly.

The preparations for Musa's pilgrimage took nine months. The story says that the king consulted his soothsayers to confirm the date when he should depart, and they said it needed to be on a Saturday that would fall on the twelfth day of a month. The exact date of Musa's pilgrimage is unknown, but he arrived in Egypt in 1324. The journey took around a year, and the written sources mention that Musa's procession numbered 60,000 men, of which 12,000 were slaves. The king provided everything needed for the long pilgrimage, and he dressed his people in the finest silk with gold ornaments. It was even said that each slave had to carry a bar of gold. Once they reached Egypt, all the slaves were sold, and the money was gifted to the Egyptians. The sultan of Egypt received 40,000 gold dinars as a gift, and much more money was shared. As stated above, the generosity of Mansa Musa was legendary.

Musa stayed in Egypt for three months before continuing his journey to the holy cities of Mecca and Medina. New slaves had to be bought for this trip. Even though the king of Mali had a number of guards, the journey across the desert and beyond Egypt was a very dangerous one. Sakura, one of the previous kings of Mali, was murdered on his way back from the Hajj, and even Mansa Musa experienced troubles of his own. His whole entourage got separated from the main caravan. The sub-Saharan people were unfamiliar with the routes that led from Cairo to Mecca, so they needed to join local caravans. On their way back to Egypt, Musa got lost and reached the seashore at Suez instead of Cairo. Before finding their way back, Musa's entourage lost around one-third of the people, as well as many animals.

On his pilgrimage, Mansa Musa went through the cities of Timbuktu and Gao, but on his way back, he annexed them and incorporated them into the Mali Empire. Timbuktu remains the most famous and mysterious city in Western Africa. Many stories were written about it, and even today, people doubt its existence. They believe it is a made-up place or a very mysterious ancient city that has yet to be discovered. However, Timbuktu is very real, and it is still inhabited. It is listed as one of the World Heritage Sites because of its importance in the Islamization of the African continent, as well as for its unique history and architecture.

Timbuktu started as a settlement in the 5th century, but its position allowed it to prosper and turn into a city. It conveniently lay on the trade routes of the Sahara region, and it became rich due to the trade in salt, ivory, and copper. Mansa Musa was able to realize the economic importance of Timbuktu, and his reputation served him well because nobody resisted the annexation of the city, which took place in either 1324 or 1325. Because of the importance of Timbuktu, Musa ordered the construction of a royal palace. This task was assigned to Ishaq al-Sahili, a Muslim architect from Spain. He built the square royal residence with a dome on the top, a design that would become a staple of the Mali Empire. The architect chose to settle in Timbuktu, and the Djinguereber Mosque, which was built there between 1324 and 1327, was attributed to him. Two centuries later, when the Songhai Empire took over the city, the mosque was torn down, and in its place, a larger one was built.

Mansa Musa also realized that the city of Timbuktu attracted many visitors because of its rich markets. Many of them were not Muslims, but they were nonetheless fascinated with the city's openness to different people. The Mali king decided to found a university there, in which Muslim scholars could preach their religion. The pious Mansa Musa saw an opportunity to utilize Timbuktu's popularity to spread Islam across Africa through its university. The city became so famous that word of it even reached Europe, and the merchants of Venice and Genoa started visiting it regularly.

Timbuktu wasn't the only city in which the Mali king opened universities. He also started Islamic studies in the cities of Djenne and Segou. But the one in Timbuktu remained one of the most popular. It quickly grew, and by the 16th century, it was able to accept over 25,000 students. Musa broadened the curriculum of the university and introduced mathematics, astronomy, and geography. Timbuktu's university became one of the largest in Africa, with a library that could be compared to the one in Alexandria.

The Power Struggle and the End of the Empire

It is unknown when exactly Mansa Musa died, but his son started appearing in the written sources as the new king of Mali in around 1337. His name was Mansa Maghan, and he ruled for only four years before he died. He didn't leave any sons capable of ruling after him, so the throne was passed to the brother of Mansa Musa, Mansa Suleyman. He was another powerful and effective ruler, although he wasn't liked among the people like his brother. While Musa was a generous king, Suleyman was inattentive. This was probably because, at this time, the Black Death had reached the northern African continent, where it killed 30 to 50 percent of its inhabitants. Although there is no evidence of plague reaching the Mali Empire, it certainly influenced trade with the north, which was one of Mali's main trading partners. The economic consequences of the Black Death were felt across the world, and the sub-Saharan kingdoms were no exception.

The information about the Mali Empire during the reign of Mansa Suleyman is plenty due to geographer Ibn Battuta, who spent eight months visiting the court in 1352/53. He witnessed the king's audiences and wrote extensively about them. He compared the richness of the Mali royal palace with the European courts, saying how they were equal in beauty and prosperity. Three hundred soldiers protected the king while he was sitting on his throne and listened to the people. The king himself was dressed in a red robe and had a golden headdress. He carried a bow and arrows with him, and just as his brother Mansa Musa, he had two horses ready to carry him wherever he needed.

Ibn Battuta also witnessed an attempt to dispose of Suleyman. The story is complicated, but it seems to have all started when the king wanted to marry a common girl named Banju instead of his first wife, Kassi. It was a tradition for the aristocracy of the Mali Empire to have many wives, but only one enjoyed the status of queen and ruled alongside her husband. For Suleyman, that was supposed to be his cousin Kassi. But he wanted to elevate the commoner Banju to that status, and so, he had to dispose of Kassi. He divorced Kassi, but she had the sympathies of other aristocrats, who offered her support. A civil war erupted between the divided people of Mali, with some supporting the king and others the ex-queen. The fighting continued until Suleyman provided the evidence that Kassi was conspiring with one of her cousins for treason. Whether this was true or not, the people of Mali agreed that it was a grave offense and that she deserved the death sentence. To avoid it, the former queen hid in a mosque. It remains unknown what happened to her in the end or if the accusations against her were true or just fabricated to serve the king's agenda.

Mansa Suleyman ruled for twenty-four years, and when he died in 1360, he was succeeded by his son Kassa. However, a civil war broke out, as the sons of Suleyman and Mansa Musa were fighting for the throne. Finally, the son of Mansa Maghan, Mari Djata II, prevailed, and he took the throne for himself. He was a tyrant who brought the empire to ruin. He was abusive toward his people, and he squandered the national treasure. He sold the gold to the Egyptians for a very low price, bringing the empire to poverty. But he didn't rule for very long. He suffered from sleeping sickness, which was transmitted by tsetse flies, and he died in 1374.

The throne was inherited by Mari Djata's son, Mansa Musa II. He wasn't at all like his father, for he was wise and fair. But he wasn't like his namesake Mansa Musa I either. Musa II was weak and unable to control his subjects. One of his advisors took control of the government for himself, and eventually, he took the throne. He is known as Mari Djata III, although he didn't belong to the royal family. He wasn't even recognized as the official king of Mali, but he controlled the throne and the government. Even though he tried his hardest to revitalize the empire after the damage caused by the civil war after Suleyman, and by the rule of the tyrant Mari Djata II, he was always seen as a usurper.

A series of weak kings followed Mansa Musa II, and all of them were unable to keep the throne for more than a few years. Various court intrigues led to assassinations and mysterious deaths until the throne was captured by Mahmud Keita, a direct descendant of the first ruler of Mali, Sunjata, in 1390. However, nothing is known about Mahmud except that he was the last ruler of Mali mentioned in the written sources. Oral tradition speaks of other kings and queens who followed but in the form of myths and legends. There is no historical evidence that could confirm their existence.

The power of the Mali Empire was undermined by the generations of the power struggle and civil wars for the throne. Soon, at the end of the 14th century, the distant kingdoms integrated into the territory of Mali broke off, and no king was strong enough to assert control and stop the dissolution of the empire. In 1433, Timbuktu was lost, as well as Gao and other distant provinces beyond the River Niger. In the 15th and 16th centuries, Gao produced powerful rulers who founded a new empire, one that would replace Mali as the powerbase of Western Africa: the Songhai Empire.

Conclusion

There are many gaps in our knowledge about ancient Africa and the kingdoms that ruled over the continent. This lack of evidence slows down our ability to learn what happened in the past. The ever-shifting sands of the Sahara Desert, as well as the probable climate changes that occurred on the continent, have hidden archaeological sites that are yet to be discovered. In the case of the mystical Land of Punt, we don't even know its exact location. However, the birthplace of humanity is a rich playground for scholars and historians, who work tirelessly to come to new conclusions and find new evidence that will part the veils that still obscure history.

Many monuments, texts, and images of the bygone days of Africa remain to be discovered, but what we already have is enough to understand the way of thinking and life of these ancient kingdoms. Egypt, a civilization that left behind so much evidence, granted us an insight into the life of other ancient lands of Africa. Through the prism of Egypt, we can learn about Nubia, Kush, and Punt. Carthage also left a rich culture behind, which still fascinates us with its stories and its connections with the rest of the world, and thanks to several ancient Roman, Greek, and Phoenician historians, we have a clear view of Carthaginian heritage.

Other kingdoms, such as Aksum, Ghana, and Mali, have rich oral traditions that can inspire our imagination. Unfortunately, the stories passed from generation to generation can rarely be confirmed with historical evidence. They remain just that, stories to be told at evening bonfires by the Berber peoples of Africa.

Luckily, the entrance of the Middle Ages brought about the Islamization of the continent. With it, many geographers, historians, and explorers of the Arab world showed interest in the African continent. They gathered witnesses who told them about the distant cities and kingdoms, such as Ghana's Koumbi Saleh and Mali's Timbuktu. They talked about the riches, about the trade routes of the Sahara Desert, of the kings and queens sitting on their ebony thrones. If not for the scholars of Islam, the history of West Africa would still be unknown to us today.

However, it's not only the lack of evidence that can be blamed for our poor knowledge of Africa's history. As the birthplace of the human race, Africa must be understood so we can better understand ourselves. Unfortunately, the archaeology of colonial times believed that the societies of ancient Africa were not capable of producing anything interesting, and at the beginning, archaeologists ignored Africa completely (except for Egypt and Carthage). Thus, excessive research on the history of this continent is just starting. And as the oldest settlement of humanity, Africa is very diverse, culturally rich, and abundant with historical information. There is so much left to discover about the first humans, their development, the first villages, cities, and kingdoms of ancient Africa. In time, more information will be discovered, as we have barely scratched the surface of the rich history of the African continent.

Here's another book by Captivating History
that you might be interested in

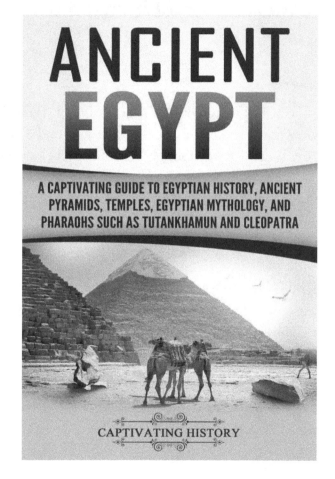

Free Bonus from Captivating History
(Available for a Limited time)

Hi History Lovers!

Now you have a chance to join our exclusive history list so you can get your first history ebook for free as well as discounts and a potential to get more history books for free! Simply visit the link below to join.

Captivatinghistory.com/ebook

Also, make sure to follow us on Facebook, Twitter and Youtube by searching for Captivating History.

References

Bard, Kathryn A. *The Wonderful Things of Punt: Excavations at a Pharaonic Harbor on the Red Sea.* Boston University, 2011.

Collins, Robert O. *Western African History.* M. Wiener Pub., 1990.

Cook, S. A. (editor), et al. *The Cambridge Ancient History: Vol 08, Rome and the Mediterranean 218-133 BC.* Publisher Not Identified, 1930.

Hatke, George. *Aksum and Nubia: Warfare, Commerce, and Political Fictions in Ancient Northeast Africa.* New York University Press, 2013.

Kendall, Timothy. *Discoveries at Sudan's Sacred Mountain of Jebel Barkal Reveal Secrets of the Kingdom of Kush.* The National Geographic Society, 1990.

László, Török. *The Kingdom of Kush Handbook of the Napatan-Meroitic Civilization.* Brill, 1997.

McBrewster, John, et al. *Mali Empire: Pre-Imperial Mali, Military History of the Mali Empire, Mandinka People, Sundiata, Keita, Musa (Mansa).* Alphascript Publishing, 2009.

Phillipson, David W. *Foundations of an African Civilisation Aksum & the Northern Horn, 1000 BC - AD 1300.* Currey, 2014.

Rollin, Charles. *Ancient History of the Egyptians, Carthaginians, Assyrians, Babylonians, Medes, and Persians, Macedonians, and Grecians, Tr. from the French, Illustrated with a New Set of Maps.* Sharpe, 1819.

Saad, Elias N. *Social History of Timbuktu: The Role of Muslim Scholars and Notables, 1400-1900.* Cambridge University Press, 2010.

Sherrow, Victoria. *Ancient Africa: Archaeology Unlocks the Secrets of Africa's Past.* National Geographic Society, 2007.